CRYPTOCURRENCY 101

The Beginner's Complete Guide to Bitcoin & Cryptocurrencies

By

Kevin Philip D. Gayao

2018

Cryptocurrency 101: The Beginner's Complete Guide to Bitcoin & Cryptocurrencies

by **Kevin Philip D. Gayao**

ISBN-13: 978-1721659005

ISBN-10: 1721659005

Cover Designer: Kurt Lee D. Gayao

Proofreaders: Jasmine Joy U. Doria and Myra G. Gahid

While the author has used good faith efforts to ensure that the information contained in this work is accurate, the author disclaims all responsibility for errors or omissions, including without limitation, responsibility for damages resulting from the use of or reliance on this work. Use of the information and instructions contained in this work is at your own risk.

Table of Contents

PREFACE

I wrote this book with the intention of helping individuals understand what cryptocurrency is all about. We have recently seen a slew of publicity, both based on facts and fiction, about cryptocurrencies notably bitcoin. Bitcoin is slowly becoming a mainstream concept primarily due to its dramatic increase in price, from less than a thousand dollars to over ten thousand dollars in less than a year. Many people made a significant windfall by merely being early believers of this 'digital asset.'

No wonder a great number of people are now interested in joining the bitcoin bandwagon! Some of those who have heard about bitcoin saw the opportunity of using the concept in their Ponzi schemes, and this is where I became very much worried. I have seen many families broken because of scams. With this book, it is my fervent desire to help prevent scams that use the concept of cryptocurrencies from ruining peoples' lives.

I believe cryptocurrency was created because of a very noble purpose and the technology behind it is incredible! This belief is the second reason why I wrote this book. I want more people to understand the economics and technology behind cryptocurrency and appreciate how it can help alleviate people's lives.

In this age of social media, it is easy to spread misinformation. I hope this book can become a reliable source of information about cryptocurrency.

KEVIN PHILIP D. GAYAO, CPA, MBA, CBP

Who should read this book?

This book is not for everyone. Although investors, traders, and programmers can find value in this book, **Cryptocurrency 101** was primarily written for persons who want to have a better appreciation and more in-depth understanding of the economics and technology behind cryptocurrencies regardless of their background. I tried my best to make this book as easy to understand as possible while careful enough not to lose critical discussions about cryptocurrency economics and technology.

In this book, I have discussed why cryptocurrency is a disruptive force that can ultimately change the way we do business today and in the near future. I have comprehensively researched the contents of this book using credible offline and online sources. I have given examples and latest statistics that can help you form an informed and sound opinion about cryptocurrency.

Finally, this book hopes to excite you with the new opportunities available to all of us, regardless of gender, status, wealth, educational attainment, culture and political beliefs. Think of the time when the internet was introduced to us in the early 1990s! We are at the forefront of another technological revolution. And, we all have an equal opportunity to learn more and be early adopters of cryptocurrency!

Guide to using this book

The first two chapters of the book tackle the circumstances that led to the creation of bitcoin, the first cryptocurrency. The second chapter expounds on the benefits of cryptocurrency.

If you want to immediately begin dealing with cryptocurrency, notably bitcoin, you can start with Chapter 5 – Dabbling in Bitcoin.

If you are already knowledgeable about the basics of cryptocurrency, you will find much value in Chapter 4 – The Value of Bitcoin and Chapter 6 – A Variety of Cryptocurrencies.

Chapter 3 (Bitcoin Demystified) discusses the amazing technology behind bitcoin.

You might also enjoy the bonus article about blockchain and smart contracts that I have included in this edition.

I suggest that you still start with the first chapter, but you can always start with any chapter and slowly immerse yourself in the enchanting world of cryptocurrencies.

The beginning of my cryptocurrency journey

I was once a skeptic. I did not believe that cryptocurrencies have real-world value.

It was in 2015 that I first used bitcoins. I was using a mobile application that uses the bitcoin network to facilitate money transfer. The app offers "bits" (1 bit is equal to 0.000001 bitcoin) as a reward to people who have performed specific tasks. Once you earned these bits, you can convert them into pesos.

I have completed those tasks and earned 500 bits (or 0.0005 bitcoin). During that time, the value of one bitcoin was ranging from $300 to $375, so the value of my bitcoins was around $0.15 to $0.20 at that time. It is not a lot, but it is still free money!

Unfortunately, there were only a few tasks where I can earn bits of bitcoins. I eventually have forgotten about the bits stored in my bitcoin wallet app. I only used the app solely for buying prepaid credits for my mobile number and my friends' mobile numbers.

Topping up using bitcoin

I was reminded of my bitcoins when I joined a startup competition in August 2016. One of the guests was the founder of the company that made the mobile app. He talked about their experience in the Philippines and their campaign to bring financial literacy to the grassroots of society. After his talk, I proudly opened that app and bragged about having it installed on my Android phone.

As I was exploring the app, I saw the value of the bits I earned in the previous years that I had forgotten. It was worth around $0.30. The value of my bitcoins more than doubled! It was then that I decided to convert my bitcoins into pesos, which I then used to buy top-up my phone credits.

I learned two things from this experience: (1) bitcoin prices are increasing, and (2) it can be used to buy something. Unfortunately, I was overwhelmed with many things back then, so I did not pursue studying bitcoins further.

Becoming a bitcoin professional

Fast forward to June 2017. While I was talking to one of my business mentors, a Singaporean real estate investor, he suddenly asked me if I have heard about bitcoins, to which I responded in the affirmative. My mentor became interested in bitcoins and cryptocurrency when one of his business associates in Singapore talked about it saying it was becoming immensely popular. He then asked me if I could invite one of our clients, who mentioned something about cryptocurrencies during one of our events, to visit us in our office and join us in our discussions.

I have contacted the client and asked him to come and talk with us. To cut the story short, we became very interested. After our late-night discussion, I decided to delve deeper into cryptocurrency.

For several months, I immersed myself in trying to learn as much as I can about cryptocurrencies especially bitcoin. I took courses on bitcoin, studied the technology behind bitcoin, and even learned how to trade bitcoins and other cryptocurrencies. Eventually, I decided to take the Certified Bitcoin Professional (CBP) exam given by the CryptoCurrency Certification Consortium (C4) based in Canada to force myself to understand the bitcoin ecosystem. I became one of the first CBPs in Southeast Asia.

The challenge ahead

More than just having the title, I consider having the CBP certificate as a challenge to help other people understand what bitcoin and cryptocurrency are all about, and how these could influence their lives. I am just a part of a small but growing community of cryptocurrency users in the country. I hope that after reading this humble work, you will join us in our advocacy to educate more people about cryptocurrencies!

Acknowledgment

This book will not be finished without the generous blessing of the Almighty, the confidence of my family and the support of my friends.

I am forever grateful to my parents, Yolanda Degay Gayao and Sergio Tacay Gayao. Without them, this humble work would have never been created. To my siblings, Keshia, Kyle Gio, Kurt Lee (who designed the cover of this book) and Katrina, thank you for the support and also for giving vital feedback about this book project.

The fantastic team behind 1Punch Inc. also made it easier for me to complete this book. It is due to their ability to keep the company running in its optimum capacity that I can finish this book.

Mainly, I am grateful to my ever-supportive business partner Thomas George L. Bumby for his enthusiasm and sage advice. I was able to find more time to write this book because of Myra Gahid's fantastic talent in management and reviewing books. It was Jasmine Joy Doria's careful eye that skimmed each page of this book to make it a lot readable. The optimism of Jeremy Magracia has helped me believe that this book is worth something. Our tech wiz Cristian Jay Duque helped me escape the routinary I.T. problems in our company that could have significantly limited my time to complete this book. Kattie Nicoleigh Belingon and Justine Louise Ferrer made sure that our company finances remain firm even without me constantly nagging them. Michael Milan's optimism and his insights have also shaped this book. Also, Julivin Alivin and Elizabeth Bumby's dynamic support in keeping 1Punch Inc. afloat has helped me concentrate on writing this book.

My sincerest gratitude as well to Raymond Lim, my business mentor, who re-introduced me to the world of cryptocurrencies.

There are a lot more people I would want to express my sincerest gratitude to, and I apologize if I am not able to mention your names here. Rest assured that even though your names are not mentioned, I will forever be grateful for your support.

Chapter 1

THE PROBLEM WITH BILLS AND COINS

"When the inhabitants of one country became more dependent on those of another, and they imported what they needed, and exported what they had too much of, money necessarily came into use."

– Aristotle

A Quick History of Money

Let us first explore how money evolved throughout the centuries to better understand why cryptocurrency was invented.

Before bills and coins were invented, humans needed to physically transfer the possession of a particular good that the other party deems as the equivalent of the good that is being given up. This system of value transfer, as we know, is quite difficult.

Imagine you are a potato farmer, and you want to eat eggs. You need to go to a chicken farmer, and give him something he wants. The chicken farmer wants potatoes. You agreed to provide one medium-sized potato for every egg, and the transaction is concluded. Assume that the chicken farmer is only willing to trade his eggs for carrots. You then look for a carrot farmer, and ask him what he wants. What if the carrot farmer also wants eggs in exchange for his carrots?

As what can be gleaned from this illustration, trading of goods without a common form of exchange is quite tricky. This direct exchange of goods is called *barter*, and this is the earliest form of trading before we had money or currency.

Eventually, our ancestors learned to exchange goods for something valuable to other people as well. You may want to trade your potatoes for salt, even though you wish for eggs, because you can easily exchange salt for eggs. In this instance, salt becomes a form of currency. Other types of prehistoric currencies include animal skins and ancient weapons.

Subsequently, coins were invented to replace prehistoric currencies. The first coins made out of metals were *minted* (the process of shaping metals into circular forms) in Lydia, now modern Turkey, in the 1100 BC. During this period, the Chinese also started using coins.

In 600 BC, the reigning rulers decided to engrave their images in the coins. This process was the beginning of a new era of currency – the *denominate*d coins. These coins have different perceived values depending on the image engraved on it.

The Chinese then invented paper money which is similar to denominated coins but in paper form. These paper notes are documentary receipts of deposits of coins used by merchants. The notes can eventually be claimed for the deposited coins at a later date. The Chinese central government eventually adopted this system, which became the norm for trade. In fact, the Chinese inscription in the paper money also warned, "All counterfeiters will be decapitated" to prevent fraud.

The Europeans noticed what the Chinese invented and also adopted the concept of paper money. European banks and private institutions started issuing bank notes, which depositors can use to exchange for precious metals like silver or gold coins. Subsequently, European governments also began issuing their own money backed by precious metals.

International trade further flourished due to the use of paper money issued by governments. Many people and institutions in Europe also started owning money issued by other governments for various reasons, and this led to the creation of the first currency (foreign exchange) market. The value of the currency was pegged to the strength of the issuing government. Thus, competing countries often tried to influence the currency of the other governments to improve their position in the international trade.

Abandoning the gold standard

For several decades, governments used gold to represent the value of the paper money that they issued. This type of money regime, called the *gold standard*, started in the United Kingdom, and eventually spread across Europe. Back then, you can be confident that the paper money you hold was backed by a proportionate amount of gold in the governments' vaults.

Why gold?

Gold was used to back money because of its intrinsic (inherent) value and usefulness:

1. There will always be a demand for gold. Gold is used in the electronics, dentistry and jewelry industries.
2. Gold is malleable and can be evenly divisible without losing value, unlike diamonds.
3. It does not spoil over time.
4. Gold can never be created and is impossible to counterfeit.
5. It has a limited supply. Only a fixed amount of gold can ever be mined on Earth.

With these characteristics, gold does not lose value. That is why gold is often called "the ultimate store of value."

However, governments soon found out that the gold mines were not producing enough, and the price of gold was not stable. As such, the gold standard has repeatedly been suspended, particularly during wartime. This suspension allowed governments to print more money to pay for their military expeditions.

After the First World War, the gold standard began to lose its appeal as a monetary regime. It further weakened when US President Franklin Delano Roosevelt criminalized the private possession of gold by individuals. This act was an attempt by the US government to control the supply of gold. As a result, the US treasury became the largest holder of gold in the world.

US-allied countries eventually used the US dollar as currency reserves rather than gold, after the US pledged to fully back the dollars with equivalent reserves of gold as part of its post-World War II commitments. So, instead of holding gold, most countries accumulated dollars.

However, the economic growth experienced by the United States in the 1960s, as well as the increasing redemption of gold for the dollar, forced President Richard Nixon to dissociate the dollar with the US gold reserves. Ultimately, the gold standard was officially abolished in 1971. Eventually, other countries followed suit.

This action resulted in a new type of monetary regime called *fiat* currency. The word *fiat* is derived from a Latin word which means "it shall be." The new monetary system implies that citizens of the country can use the particular type of paper, usually printed with beautiful designs and bearing unique anti-counterfeit features, as a representation of value because the government says so. Another term for *fiat currency* is *legal tender*.

Losing the value of money

The emergence of fiat currency has helped governments support the growth of their economies. Governments no longer needed to be shackled by a limited supply of gold to control the supply of money. Central banks, like the *US Federal Reserve*, have better control over fiat currency supply because it is not a scarce or a fixed resource like gold. This feature of the fiat currency regime gives central banks the power to manage economic variables such as credit supply, liquidity, interest rates and money velocity.

Essentially, a series of wrong decisions made by a central bank can lead to a broken economy. Many economists agree that the 2008 financial crisis was a result of the US Federal Reserve's inability to manage the risks in the housing loan market, some experts argued, though, that having a fiat currency regime helped reduce the impact of the financial crisis.

Although fiat currency regimes and strong central banks have many advantages, they also carry some risks. One of the significant risks associated with having fiat currency is the fact that fiat currency can become worthless due to loss of trust.

Money versus Currency

Earlier in this chapter, I used the terms "money" and "currency" interchangeably. However, I want to make a quick distinction. Money and currency are similar because they are used as mediums of exchange and units of account. Both share the same characteristics such as divisibility and interchangeability. The big difference lies in the fact that only money is backed by precious metals (i.e., gold). Money, therefore, has intrinsic (inherent) value while currency derives its value from the trust provided by the government. Without trust in the government, the currency becomes worthless.

For the rest of this book, I will be using these terms with the above distinction in mind.

A hypothetical scenario

Imagine a government that needs a massive amount of money to recover from a natural disaster, which severely affected their economy. Politicians do not want to impose additional taxes on their citizens, so they decide to borrow money from neighboring countries and to print more money (currency). The economy quickly recovered, and the politicians rejoiced. However, inflation became a major problem because there is so much money in circulation. *Inflation* refers to the increase in the prices of goods and services primarily brought about by increased purchasing power of the population and the rise in money supply.

Since their local currency started to lose its purchasing power because of rising commodity prices, the citizens preferred to store their wealth in another currency (e.g., the US dollar). The population began to lose faith in their government because of its failure to control inflation.

A few years after recovery, the economy is in distress. The prices of basic goods continued to increase. Many banks and financing institutions went bankrupt since their loans lost a lot of value and people stopped making deposits. People started transferring their wealth to 'safer' assets, such as other currencies and gold. The value of the local currency is quickly decreasing, and the government can no longer pay its debt.

This scenario, also known as *hyperinflation*, may seem far from happening in many developed and developing nations, but it has happened numerous times in history. There have been over 58 episodes of hyperinflation in the past 100 years.

A more recent incident of hyperinflation is happening in Venezuela. The country, which was once the wealthiest country in Latin America, has experienced an unprecedented increase in their inflation rates. Many Venezuelans no longer trust in their currency, the *bolivar*, pushing them to start buying dollars and bitcoin. As of this writing, their current inflation rate is nearing 50 percent. Some experts estimate that this level has already been breached, and there is a possibility for the *bolivar* to become worthless soon. (*Note: The Venezuelan government has issued their asset-backed cryptocurrency, called the "Petro," to address this issue.*)

The need for a solution

One major problem discussed in this chapter is the possibility of fiat currency to lose its value. The primary factors that can lead to this devaluation of currency are the unabated printing of currency which is a direct result of the abandonment of the gold standard, the lack of trust in the government, and the resulting hyperinflation.

The incessant printing of US dollars resulted in the dollar losing over 83 percent of its value. To put this into perspective, you need $616.65

today to purchase the same amount of goods worth $100 in 1971. That is how you 'passively' lose the value of your money.

Since returning to the gold standard is not entirely feasible, economists have been trying to find a viable solution to this problem.

In 2008, Satoshi Nakamoto offered a possible solution to this modern economic problem.

Key Points

1. Money has a rich history.
2. Currency was developed when the gold standard was abandoned.
3. Currency is based on trust. Once that trust is broken, the currency becomes worthless.
4. The devaluation of our currency results in inflation which is a major problem.

Evolution of Money

> **Direct Trade**
> *Barter*

Ancient times

> **Early forms of money**
> *Salt, animal skin, weapons*

1100 B.C.

> **Use of Precious Metals**
> *Minted coins and
> denominated coins*

600 B.C.

> **Asset-backed Paper Money**
> *Documentary receipts &
> bank notes*

1970s

——— Gold Standard Abandoned ———

> **Fiat Currency**
> Bills and coins, e-money

2009

> **Cryptocurrency**
> *Bitcoin*

Chapter 2

THE NEXT GENERATION CURRENCY

"The swarm is headed towards us."

– Satoshi Nakamoto, Creator of Bitcoin

Greed and crisis

The 2008 global financial crisis has been considered "the worst economic crisis" since the Great Depression in 1929. Human greed was seen as the cause of this crisis.

U.S. banks provided housing loans to individuals with high-risk credit – people who may not be able to complete payment of the loan. The houses were used as collateral. To protect themselves from the possibility that the borrowers would default on their loans, they transferred the risk to other financial institutions through a financial product called a *derivative*. They are called *derivatives* because they derive their value from the underlying asset, in this case, the houses.

These *derivatives* were eventually sold to other financial institutions, investment, and pension funds. To protect their investments in the *derivatives*, the banks took out a form of insurance called *credit default swap* from the American International Group (AIG), which was once a major American insurance company.

For years, executives of the banks involved in this scheme enjoyed substantial bonuses because of profits that were booked from the high-risk housing loans.

Unexpectedly, many people who took out the loans eventually defaulted and the banks took possession of the houses. The problem was that the prices of the repossessed homes were quite low because of the real estate bubble popping. Due to the drop in the real estate market, it became clear that the *derivatives* bought by other financial institutions were overvalued or even worthless.

Initially, the banks and financial institutions were confident that they were protected from the defaults in the housing loans market because of the insurance they took from AIG. However, AIG did not have sufficient cash to pay out all claims. Consequently, a global financial panic ensued.

As the saying goes, "when the U.S. sneezes, the world catches a cold." These events led to the 2009 global depression which resulted to a staggering 6 to 14 trillion dollars' worth of lost value. Until today (2018), we are still in the process of recovering from this crisis.

Governments were powerless in trying to cushion the impact of the crisis. Millions of people lost their homes, their jobs, and even their lives. People thought that their governments, through the enforcement of laws, could protect their wealth and prevent financial crises from happening. They thought that their governments could also protect them from greedy individuals who are part of the financial system. People thought that their governments have safety nets in place to ensure that what may be lost in a crisis can be recovered. However, it is apparent that even governments with the best minds can be helpless against a financial mess of such magnitude and global scale.

To quickly reduce the impact of the crisis and to keep the financial system afloat, governments had to bail out these banks by printing more currency. This action resulted to the further devaluation of fiat currency – the dollar, euro, and yen. Even the public became burdened with more taxes due to the debt that the government had to shoulder to bail out the banks – the same banks with officers whose greed and recklessness caused the crisis.

Frustrated over the failure of human organizations to temper greed and to prevent a similar crisis from happening, Satoshi Nakamoto invented Bitcoin – the first cryptocurrency. Nakamoto wanted to put a stop to the cycle of greed and crisis.

In this chapter, we will discuss how cryptocurrencies can usher the way to a new world order where value is not at the mercy of a few groups' whims.

It is an issue of trust

The current fiat monetary regime relies heavily on trust in the government. This trust extends to the financial system which includes the banks. Essentially, you can only do transactions with other people because you trust the pillars of the financial system.

We work hard because we believe that the money that our employers pay us have value. We think it has value because the government says so. The reason we let institutions, like banks, manage our hard-earned money is because we trust them. We accept payment via checks for our goods and services because we trust the person who issued the check and we believe the drawee bank will honor the check. Checks are another form of paper currency if duly-authorized.

We use credit cards because we put so much trust in credit card companies. When we buy something online, we often use our credit cards because credit card companies have mechanisms that could protect the buyer and merchant. If the merchant does not deliver the product, then we can ask the credit company to reverse the transaction, so we do not get charged for something that was not delivered. Merchants, on the other hand, are also willing to accept credit card payments because they trust the credit card companies to deposit the amount owed by the customer to their bank accounts.

Can you imagine a world where you cannot trust anyone to manage your funds? What if your bank goes bankrupt and closes down?

*The five dollar bill. Upon closer inspection, the following phrase can be read: "**THIS NOTE IS LEGAL TENDER FOR ALL DEBTS, PUBLIC AND PRIVATE.**" The US Federal Reserve is willing to meet the debt obligations created by the issuance of the US dollar. This means that holders can also meet their debt obligations for goods and services via the denomination on the currency. The US Federal Reserve assures holders that the paper note has value because it guarantees its value.*

The cost of trust

Our trust-based economy has worked fine for decades because it is effective. It has helped grow a very robust economy. The big problem is when that trust is lost, our 'money' also loses value (as we have discussed in the previous chapter). When this happens, everyone will be hesitant in using his or her paper currency to transact. No one will want to use or accept a worthless piece of paper. Thus, the government and financial institutions take great pains to ensure that the public will continue trusting them. However, maintaining a trust-based economy does not come cheap.

Central banks would have to continually monitor what is happening in the economy to make informed decisions, craft monetary policies and regulate other banks, so they hire top-notch professionals. The banks also have to develop their systems to ensure that they comply with the central bank's regulations and maintain top-of-the-line systems to protect their clients. They invest in the latest security devices, both online and offline, to ensure their clients are protected. Banks have to avail the services of escrow companies to enable payments between merchants and buyers. Fees have to be paid to settle disputes between parties. Credit card companies, whose services are also tapped by banks, invest in the latest transaction processing and security technologies to maintain their ability to serve their clients.

Have you noticed that most banks always come up with advertisements highlighting the fact that you can 'trust' them with your money, that they have been there for a long time, or that they have the best customer service? These marketing strategies also add to the costs that trust-based economy participants have to pay.

The costs involved in keeping this trust-based ecosystem healthy are quite significant, and end-users have no other option but to pay.

Throughout history, however, we have seen many banks close for various reasons. One usual reason why banks close is mismanagement resulting in insolvency. Protective systems that run free from human intervention are only effective up to a certain degree. Human actions can easily override systems, and humans can sometimes commit mistakes that can ultimately lead to the erosion of trust.

In almost all cases of bank closures, depositors will only recover a portion of the money that they had deposited through a tedious claiming process. The failure of banks illustrates the possibility of losing the value of money which may happen in a trust-based economy despite the strict regulation of central banks.

Eliminating the need for centralized trust

The world experienced the worst global financial crisis in 2008 which primarily resulted from the failure of the U.S. government to regulate their banks and other financial institutions. The subsequent depression is a perfect example of the loss of value wherein there is a breakdown of trust within the financial system. Though it may be difficult to compute for the actual value lost from the 2008 crisis, it is estimated that the world lost around **6 to 14 trillion** dollars in less than one year.

During this time, Satoshi Nakamoto, an anonymous person or group, released a 9-page whitepaper entitled "Bitcoin: A Peer-to-Peer Electronic Cash System." The whitepaper outlined the technical aspects of what is now known as bitcoin – the world's first commercially-used cryptocurrency.

Fed up with the imperfections of the trust-based, centralized economy, Nakamoto proposed a new financial paradigm that eliminated the need to trust systems developed by imperfect, and sometimes irrational, humans. Bitcoin does not rely on *centralized* trust or trust that is given to a few people working within the financial system. Nakamoto suggested the use of technology and cryptographic proof that allows people to directly transact with each other without the need to trust another party (i.e., banks and other financial institutions). This system is known as *decentralized* trust, which is trust that is dependent on a network of *peers*. A *decentralized* system is a unique scheme where no individual or group of users make decisions for everyone.

Who is Satoshi Nakamoto?

Back in 2008, Satoshi Nakamoto claimed to be a 36-year-old male Japanese programmer. After launching bitcoin in January 2009, and actively developing the code for a few years, he suddenly disappeared from the internet in April 2011. He said that he was moving on to other things.

Dan Kaminsky, a leading internet-security expert, who examined the bitcoin code, concluded that Satoshi Nakamoto was "a world-class programmer with a deep understanding of the C++ programming language, and who also understands economics, cryptography and peer-to-peer networking." He further said that "either there's a team of people who worked on this or this guy is a genius."

In honor of his contributions to the cryptocurrency revolution, the smallest unit of bitcoin was named after Nakamoto. One *satoshi* is equivalent to one hundred millionth of a single bitcoin (0.00000001 BTC).

Satoshi's anonymity often raised unjustified concerns founded on the lack of understanding of bitcoin's open-source nature. The software behind bitcoin is published openly, and any developer around the world can review the code or make their own modified version of the software. Satoshi's influence was limited to the changes he made being adopted by others, and therefore he does not have control over bitcoin. As such, Satoshi Nakamoto's identity is probably "as relevant today as the identity of the person who invented paper."

Why trust cryptocurrencies?

I will briefly discuss here the three main reasons why we can trust cryptocurrencies:

1. **The absence of *centralized* trust.** Bitcoin and most cryptocurrencies are *decentralized*, meaning they are not controlled by any central authority (or government) headed by a group of people who may be imperfect, irrational or motivated by greed. Decentralization enables us to transfer value without going through costly intermediaries. This means we have complete control over our money.

2. **Protected from devaluation.** When talking about cryptocurrencies, it is essential that we talk about the underlying economics. The supply of bitcoin and other cryptocurrencies have already been predetermined even before the first transaction. By putting a cap on the total number of cryptocurrency in circulation, users can be assured that it will not suffer devaluation. As more people use cryptocurrency, the demand will also increase. The price will naturally rise following the law of supply and demand.

3. **Powered by an innovative technology.** *Blockchain*, which is one of the underlying technologies behind bitcoin and other cryptocurrencies, is a disruptive invention that uses cryptographic technology to ensure the integrity of the decentralized, peer-to-peer (P2P) network. Aside from being highly-secure, the *blockchain* is fully-transparent and is based on sound mathematical principles. Many experts agree that the technology behind bitcoin is the real deal. They have even likened the *blockchain* technology to the internet.

More on the blockchain technology in Chapter 3.

Though I have listed only three main reasons why you can place your trust in cryptocurrencies, you may find more reasons as you go through the remaining pages of this book.

Cryptography + Currency = Cryptocurrency

We have earlier covered the concepts related to the word "currency" in this book. The term *currency* implies the utility and usage of cryptocurrencies while the word *cryptography* refers to the enabling technology of cryptocurrencies.

Blockchain technology, which is one of the core technologies behind cryptocurrencies, makes use of cryptographic techniques. In this section, we will quickly tackle cryptography and its application in cryptocurrency.

So what is cryptography?

Cryptography (or *cryptology*) is defined as the practice and study of techniques for secure communication in the presence of third parties. In simpler terms, *cryptography* is a method for sending hidden messages.

Let us say you want to send a secret message to another person. The message is something valuable like the secret recipe of your favorite fried chicken. You place it in a sealed envelope and have it sent via courier to the intended recipient. However, there is the risk that another person, who is also interested in the secret message, will open the envelope and steal the secret recipe.

A safer way to transfer the message is to convert the message into a 'puzzle,' and give it to a messenger who will deliver it to the intended recipient. You have designed the puzzle in such a way that only the recipient can solve it. Both you and the recipient understand how to solve the puzzle because you agreed upon the solution process during your last meeting. In this case, the messenger (or anyone for that matter) will not be able to understand your message and will have less motivation to try and steal the secret recipe because of the difficulty required to solve the puzzle.

The previous illustration is a basic example of the early application of cryptography. The sender *encrypts* a message using some mathematical puzzle, which the recipient can then *decrypt* using a predefined set of rules or processes (algorithm). Modern cryptography is heavily based on mathematical theory and computer science. The mathematical puzzles or *cryptographic algorithms* used are created by complex mathematics that require the use of computers. This process makes these puzzles very difficult to solve, which makes it hard for anyone to figure out the secret message. Since the advent of computers, the various tools used to carry out cryptography have become increasingly sophisticated and its application more widespread. Applications of modern cryptography include e-commerce, chip-based payment cards, computer passwords, military communication, and cryptocurrencies.

Actually, cryptocurrency technology does not involve the sending of secret messages because most of their transactions are made public. How, then, does cryptography come into the picture? Cryptocurrency technologies, just like the paradigm proposed by Nakamoto for bitcoin, use cryptographic techniques particularly hashing and digital signatures.

Hashing and Digital Signatures

Cryptocurrencies use *hashing* as a means to verify data integrity. *Hashing* is the process of converting a variable length data to a fixed-length string of data. In other words, *hashing* is a process of taking information that is readable by humans and making it into something that makes no sense at all using a mathematical function.

Here is an example of hashing output using *SHA-256*, one of the commonly-used hashing functions, which produces a 32-byte data string:

Input	Output
I love you	c33084feaa65adbbbebd0c9bf292a26ffc6dea9 7b170d88e501ab4865591aafd
I love you very much!	91e6d11df1d6a2d29e7a26814cd590790e10df c20abf9e8065c951a59f0872a1

The output is called a *hash* which looks like a random set of letters and numbers. The same *hash* (output) will always result from the same input, but modifying the data (input), by even one bit, will completely change the *hash*. *Hashing* is used in bitcoin and other cryptocurrencies to:

(a) maintain the blockchain – the underlying technology used by cryptocurrencies (more on this subject later);

(b) encode users' addresses (private and public keys); and

(c) mine / validate cryptocurrency transactions.

On the other hand, the use of *digital signatures* in cryptocurrencies was derived from a traditional cryptographic technology called *Elliptic Curve Cryptography*. Mathematically-derived digital signatures allow a user to 'sign' transactions. A valid *digital signature* gives a recipient proof that the message:

(a) was created by a known sender (authentication);

(b) that the sender cannot deny having sent the message (non-repudiation); and

(c) that the message was not altered in transit (integrity).

The topic of *hashing* and *digital signatures* is a very complicated subject matter and is beyond the scope of this book. However, you need to understand that the use of *hashing* and *digital signatures*, which were derived from cryptography and were carefully embedded with other technologies, ushered the birth of bitcoin and cryptocurrencies.

Cryptography is indeed an impressive technological innovation that is now disrupting how the world does business.

Cryptocurrency: The next generation money

So far, we have discussed the need to solve the problem of fiat currency by replacing trust with cryptographic proof.

Cryptography provides security and authentication within the network as well as undeniable proof that transactions occurred within the network. It makes the blockchain devoid of human interaction making the system consistently rational.

Let us now define cryptocurrency.

My most straightforward definition of a *cryptocurrency* is a **currency in digital form that is secured by cryptography.**

It is a type of currency, which means that it is used as a medium of exchange and not backed by precious metal like gold or other types of physical assets. Cryptocurrencies also reside online, so it does not have any physical form. Moreover, the entire cryptocurrency network is made secure using high-level cryptography.

A more technical definition would describe *cryptocurrency* as validated transaction entries in an online public **database** or ledger which is secured by cryptography that cannot be changed without fulfilling specific conditions.

Cryptocurrency is just like your funds in any bank. You can check the balance of your account, transfer them to another account, and pay bills using your bank's online platform or mobile app. When you pay bills online, you do not physically see money being transferred between your bank and the merchant's bank but you can see that your account balance is immediately updated. Everything happens without the need for you to withdraw cash from an ATM and personally give your money to the merchant. The bank simply took note of your authorized transactions, updated their database, and settled everything at a particular point in time.

In the previous example, there was an exchange of value between you and the merchant which happened online because you trusted the bank's online systems to be safe and secure. Your account was immediately updated to reflect your balance. The bank processed the transaction by updating their central **database** which cannot be changed without proper authorization.

Basically, cryptocurrency platforms function similarly to online banking systems. There is just one big difference – you do not need a bank or a financial institution to enable your transactions.

Why use cryptocurrency?

If banks can already do what cryptocurrencies can, then why use cryptocurrencies?

I will go through some of the problems with the existing system and discuss how cryptocurrency tries to solve these problems.

1. Cryptocurrencies are decentralized.

The contents of a database are stored in the memory and disk of a particular computer system. Anybody with sufficient access to that system, including external attackers, can destroy or corrupt the data within the system. The moment you entrust your data to a *centralized database*, you also become dependent on the human organization that keeps and controls such database.

The recent failures of some banks in preventing hacking incidents illustrate the single point of failure of centralized databases. Whether the failure is due to programming errors, unauthorized access, physical hardware damage, hacking (cyber-theft), or simple human negligence, the systems connected to the central database will not work or will be compromised. The failure of the centralized database can cause some severe problems to the users and erodes the trust given to the entire banking industry.

In *decentralized* databases used in cryptocurrencies, this scenario cannot happen. No central authority controls the entire network's database. Instead, special members of a cryptocurrency network called *nodes* maintain copies of the database. This means that even if 99.9 percent of all network participants were destroyed, attacked, or had withdrawn from the cryptocurrency network, you can still transact as long as a member of the network has a copy of the decentralized database or public ledger. This type of decentralization also prevents the creation of fictitious transactions, since you need to convince the majority of the network participants to believe that your transaction is valid.

Bitcoin's blockchain introduced the concepts of *consensus rules* and *proof-of-work algorithm* which makes it possible to validate transactions even without a central authority. You will learn more about this topic when we discuss *blockchain*.

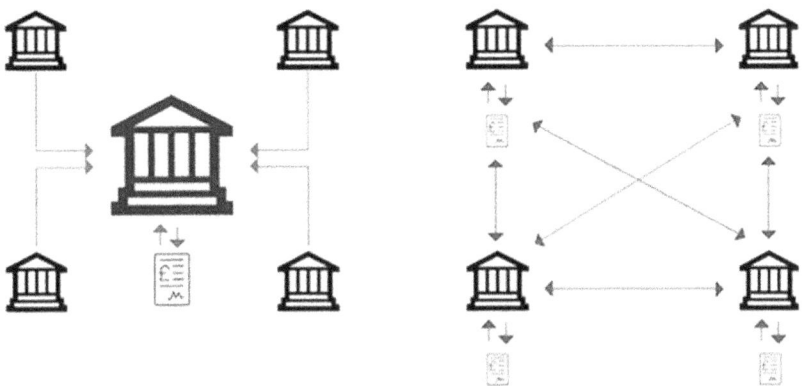

The picture shows the difference between the network structure in a centralized network (left) vs a decentralized network (right). Image by Alejandro Reyes (Michigan Blockchain Community)

2. Cryptocurrencies are inherently secure.

One of the first tasks I do when I purchase a brand new computer is to install a third-party antivirus application. Most people do this to protect their computer from computer viruses or malware which can compromise the files or even the user's personal information. Banks often install topnotch security software to protect their clients' information. Breaches in banks' network security usually result in the leakage of clients' private information and their accounts.

Some hackers may even modify details of accounts, create fictitious transactions, or even steal funds from the bank.

Current database infrastructure does not have built-in cryptography unlike cryptocurrencies. The underlying technology of cryptocurrencies makes use of cryptography to secure the entire network. Cryptography enables automated error-checking and validation. This means that even without a third-party application, the whole network is protected from hackers and fake transactions.

Theoretically-speaking, it is possible to mount an attack to steal cryptocurrencies or create fictitious transactions. However, the amount that is required to make this attack possible is staggering. The cryptography built in the blockchain makes it extremely difficult to hack the network. Currently, analysts estimate that you need at least $30 billion to modify previous transactions and create a fake bitcoin. Instead of trying to alter the database and create a single bitcoin, hackers might instead be more interested in legally buying bitcoin!

Are cryptocurrencies safe?

One of the major concerns for many cryptocurrency spectators is security. They have heard news of cryptocurrency exchanges and wallets being hacked, and cryptocurrencies were stolen.

Let me be clear. The technology behind cryptocurrency – the protocol and the cryptography – has a strong security track record. Cryptocurrency networks are very secure. In fact, there have been no known breaches in the bitcoin network since its inception in 2009.

So, what is with all the hacking incidents involving cryptocurrencies? Most security breaches related to cryptocurrencies are from the services that connect the cryptocurrency network (protocol). These include centralized cryptocurrency exchanges, wallets, and other applications connected to the network. Cyber-criminals take advantage of weaknesses in the security systems employed by these network participants.

The same techniques that cyber-criminals employ to target bank clients are also used to target cryptocurrency users. One of the most common methods used in breaching security systems is sending phishing emails that contain a computer virus or malicious software that can collect usernames and passwords.

The risk of your cryptocurrencies being stolen is similar to the risk of your funds being taken from a bank account. However, since bank services do not come cheap, it is still possible to recover your stolen funds. For cryptocurrency, it is nearly impossible to do so.

We will discuss how to keep your cryptocurrencies safe in a later chapter. However, for now, rest assured that there are sufficient and practical ways to protect your cryptocurrency from theft.

3. Cryptocurrencies are fast and global.

Have you ever experienced sending money to a loved one abroad? Alternatively, have you tried receiving money from someone outside of the country? If you wish to transfer funds from outside the country, you have to wait for 1 to 5 days before your bank or remittance agent confirms the transaction. Only then can your loved one be able to withdraw the funds. The speed by which the transaction is processed usually depends on the fee you are willing to pay.

In comparison, it only takes a couple of minutes to confirm fund transfers using cryptocurrencies because of the underlying technology. With just a few clicks of your mobile phone or laptop, your fund transfer is immediately broadcasted to the cryptocurrency network, confirmed by special network participants, and delivered to the recipient's address in a few minutes. Since there are no additional intermediaries involved (i.e., bank networks, remittance agents, and money changers), you can be assured that there will be no undue delays in your transaction ensuring that your loved ones will receive the funds promptly. You do not have to deal with delays due to system maintenance, cyber-theft, or any database errors.

Remember, cryptocurrencies are powered by potentially millions of shared computers so there is no possibility of the network experiencing a downtime. Moving funds can now be done more efficiently without the need for banks or remittance agents!

4. Cryptocurrency transactions are cheaper.

Depending on where the funds will be coming from, the remittance fees or service charges collected by the remittance agent or bank vary. The fee can range from $10 to $128 for every $1,000 sent with a transfer time of 1 to 5 days. To be fair, banks and remittance companies need numerous people and processes in place to prevent their central databases from being compromised. The need for security requires hiring, setting up operations, and maintaining the system. These processes take significant time and money as discussed earlier.

Blockchain offers a way to replace these centralized authorities (banks and remittance agents) with technology maintained by *peers* and secured by ingenious cryptography. Blockchain uses the increasing capacity of computer systems to provide a new way of replacing humans and other less efficient technologies with better technologies. Think about cars replacing horse carriages, smartphones replacing telephones, and Wikipedia replacing those heavy encyclopedia sets. Blockchain technology tends to be substantially cheaper to maintain once it has been tested and checked for errors.

A small transaction fee is charged by the cryptocurrency network. This fee is paid to special network participants, called *miners*, who help validate transactions. These transaction fees are usually fixed, so you do not have to worry about the fee increasing as you send higher amounts of money.

5. Cryptocurrency transactions are private and transparent.

Will you give a complete stranger your personal information that is linked to your bank account or credit card? You will most probably answer no. However, this is what happens when you transact with banks and other intermediaries. You are left with no choice but to entrust them with your personal information which they can use to facilitate transactions with other banks or financial intermediaries.

There are rational reasons for giving your personal information to institutions. Primarily, it is to prevent criminals from making use of the financial system to 'launder' funds from illegal activities. Moreover, it allows the government to monitor changes in your wealth for taxation purposes.

When using cryptocurrency networks, your privacy is protected. One of the main reasons for the creation of bitcoin is to enable peer-to-peer transactions without the need to provide your personal information. Similar to using paper currency, you can pay someone without knowing the other party. You also do not have to provide your personal information to the other party. Imagine a world where you are required to provide all your personal and contact information to pay a vendor in the market. This system will be impractical and might pose security concerns.

In the cryptocurrency world, you are assigned a public *address* where people can send cryptocurrencies to. Think of the address as your bank account number. You can give your bank account number to anyone who wants to deposit funds into your account without compromising the security of your account.

The addresses which look like a string of alphanumeric characters are generated using an application or program called a *wallet*. This is an example of a bitcoin address:

1ELoBhd6mP8qU5kLqvjn8Ztue16x1YQvXN

Anyone can create an address. You are not required to fill-out forms. Unless you publicly reveal your identity, you alone know the cryptocurrencies you own and the transactions you made using cryptocurrencies.

Why information privacy matters

It is the right of every individual to be able to protect their personal data. The choice to act anonymously or privately should relatively be at our discretion.

Our personal information is critical especially when these are used by people to make decisions. These information define our personal and professional reputations. When getting a loan from a bank, applying for a job, or taking a national examination, our data is collected, stored, and used to determine our qualifications. Our personal data can even determine what we see on the internet (e.g., ads). Thus, it is essential that we have a way to access, correct, or update our data. Otherwise, we become completely helpless in how other people and institutions interact with us based on personal information previously collected with or without our knowledge.

It is terrifying to realize that despite the freedom we enjoy, important decisions that can affect our lives may be based on gathered information without our participation or awareness.

This issue of privacy leads me to the next topic – *transparency*. All transactions in most cryptocurrency networks are recorded in a *public ledger*. This means that transactions since the establishment of the cryptocurrency are traceable and permanently stored in the decentralized network. The level of transparency in the network eliminates the need for centralized authorities and intermediaries to 'reconcile' their records. It also ensures that only valid transactions are recorded in the public ledger. Anyone who wants to modify previously recorded transactions or to introduce fictitious transactions will have difficulty in convincing the watchful eyes of basically everyone in the network. This unique way of recording transactions using the blockchain is one of the revolutionary techniques introduced by Satoshi Nakamoto and will be discussed in succeeding chapters.

As long as no one can connect your identity to an address, you enjoy a degree of privacy. In the event that you reveal your ownership of a cryptocurrency address, anyone can trace all your transactions from the time you have joined the network. You then lose your privacy. This is the case for bitcoin which is known as a 'pseudonymous' cryptocurrency. Thus, protecting your privacy becomes your primary responsibility.

Is bitcoin the criminal's currency?

Many prominent persons in the financial world and various governments have expressed alarm over the use of bitcoin because of the anonymous nature of the transactions within the network. They say that bitcoin can be used by criminals to hide or 'cleanse' (launder) their loot from criminal activities.

It is true that bitcoin has been previously used by criminals, particularly cyber-criminals, to collect their ransom and hide their money while remaining anonymous. However, it is becoming harder to stay anonymous in the bitcoin network. This is because of know-your-customer (KYC) procedures imposed by regulators and other self-regulation measures adopted by bitcoin wallet providers. KYC procedures require the user to provide multiple proofs of identity including a copy of a valid identification card, passport or a bill with the user's name and home address.

As mentioned, once your identity has been successfully linked to a particular bitcoin address your entire transaction history can quickly be revealed. It will be difficult for you to deny those transactions since you alone have the digital signature to authorize transactions from your wallet.

In fact, law enforcers around the world have been analyzing the bitcoin blockchain to successfully arrest elusive criminals involved in illicit activities including ransomware attacks (a form of extortion), hacking, online drug sales, money laundering, and sex trafficking.

Since remaining anonymous using the bitcoin network is becoming more and more difficult, criminals have shifted to using other cryptocurrencies, like *Zcash*, *Dash*, and *Monero*, which are designed to conceal the identity of the transacting parties.

Similar to money and the internet, bitcoin and most cryptocurrencies are merely tools for human usage. As tools, they can be used for good or evil. However, the economic and technological benefits of cryptocurrency cannot be denied even for law enforcement. The cryptocurrencies that criminals use to hide their identity can also be used to expose them.

6. Cryptocurrency does not require backups.

Losing critical personal documents in your computer due to hardware or software failure is troublesome. Banks, which handle hundreds of thousands of transactions that are worth several millions or even billions, may spell their doom when they fail to create backups.

Regular backups, whether manual or automatic, is a standard procedure in maintaining database systems. In case something unexpected happens, the files can be restored and there will be no service disruptions. However, the need to regularly create backups poses a big concern for centralized databases.

In decentralized databases, the creation of backups is no longer needed. The fact that multiple copies of the same database is synchronized, and validated using an innovative technology by many participants of the network, eliminates the need to create a backup. The creation of database backups is inherent in the network.

Consequently, there will never be a downtime for backups or 'maintenance' in decentralized databases making the network always available. There is also no danger of potentially losing or corrupting data.

Banks and other non-financial institutions are actually looking at using blockchain technology to create backups for their centralized databases. Utilizing the blockchain adds resiliency and flexibility to bank networks by providing accurate and cryptographically-secured transaction history.

Global Impact of Cryptocurrencies

In this chapter, we have already discussed the solution offered by cryptocurrency to the pervasive trust problem that can result in the devaluation of fiat currency. The idea behind cryptocurrency is to replace trust in centralized structures that are controlled by human organizations with technology that is heavily based on cryptography. We have also tackled the reasons why cryptocurrency is a viable alternative to our bills and coins.

Before we proceed to the next chapter, let me go through the possible impacts of cryptocurrency to our world.

1. A peer-to-peer electronic payment system

The process of global payments will just be like physically handing over bills and coins to another party. You do not need to provide your personal information to pay someone over the internet. You do not need to apply for a bank account and go through a tedious credit investigation to be able to transact online. You can pay anyone and receive payment wherever you are located. This can increase transactions between individuals regardless of their background. Whether you are a farmer from a developing country trying to sell your product to someone located thousands of kilometers away, a mother who is a victim of war trying to sell your wares online, or an elementary student trying to sell custom-made shirts using social media, individuals can do business without going through costly, and often discriminatory, intermediaries.

Cryptocurrency can undoubtedly become an alternative currency. Cryptocurrency will become fiat currencies' biggest rival.

2. Decentralization and deregulation of currency

The tendency of central banks to abuse their authority to print 'money' has resulted to the birth of cryptocurrency. The use of cryptocurrencies removes the need to trust central authorities. Individuals can freely transact with one another without fear that their money will be devalued or seized.

The decentralized nature of cryptocurrencies also makes it difficult for governments to regulate the use of cryptocurrencies. Without a central authority that manages and houses the central servers of the network, governments will find it challenging to impose their demands on the network participants.

Regulators, as part of their mandate, will undoubtedly try to enforce know-your-customer (KYC) procedures on cryptocurrency exchanges, storage providers, and individuals or institutions dealing with cryptocurrencies. Regulators do this to prevent money laundering and other illicit activities. However, controlling the network participants do not equate to controlling the entire network which is composed of individuals and groups that are located in various states in the world.

Currency regulation and cryptocurrencies

Governments have regularly controlled their currencies to protect their political and economic interests which may not necessarily benefit their citizens.

Residents of countries that have isolationist tendencies, like North Korea, cannot receive crucial funds from relatives in other countries. If they can receive funds, the funds would have been significantly reduced because of transaction fees and other charges.

China has heavily regulated their currency to protect their economic interest. They impose measures to control the movement of cash outside the country. Chinese entrepreneurs and investors who want to expand their operations and diversify their holdings have limited capacity to do so because of government restrictions.

The crackdown on illegal activities in countries like India and Venezuela, through *demonetization*, has resulted to the devaluation of their currencies. *Demonetization* is a government act that declares a currency, either wholly or partially, no longer be accepted as legal tender, thus rendering it worthless. The demonetization of certain denominations of the currency in India and Venezuela has resulted in the shortfall of cash and subsequent economic slowdown.

These events that happened in recent years have boosted the use of cryptocurrencies, notably bitcoin, by residents of these countries. Cryptocurrencies enabled residents of the aforementioned countries to still be able to transact with other people without government intervention.

3. **The creation and reinvention of new industries**

The creation of cryptocurrency ushered the birth of an entirely new industry that supports cryptocurrency. New companies were created because of the need for specialist developers who can build decentralized applications (DApps) or peer-to-peer software that runs using the blockchain without the need for a central server.

Another industry that cryptocurrency helped revitalize is the hardware industry, particularly those that create *application-specific integrated circuits* (ASIC). An ASIC is a type of integrated circuit (IC) that has been specially repurposed for cryptocurrency mining (See Chapter 3 on the topic of Mining). This type of computer hardware cannot be used for general purpose computing.

Although banks and other financial intermediaries (remittance companies) are seen to be the services that will be primarily affected by the growth of cryptocurrencies, many experts believe that other traditional businesses can also be significantly impacted. Industries that make heavy use of centralized databases or systems can be changed. Some of the changes that may happen to existing industries are:

- More prevalent use of cryptography in cybersecurity,
- Record-keeping and credentials management in schools and other institutions of learning,
- Introduction of blockchain voting solutions to potentially eliminate voter fraud and manipulation,
- Secure and public implementation of contracts,
- Identity management using cryptography and blockchain technologies,
- The use of smart content for intellectual property rights management for the entertainment industry,
- Tokenization of physical properties and recording over an immutable public ledger,
- Improved health records management and sharing, and
- Secured, decentralized cloud storage of files.

These are just some of the possible changes that are expected within traditional industries. Some of these innovations are actively developed and promoted by startups run by young developers and entrepreneurs. In other industries these innovative thrusts are led by industry experts that believe in what cryptocurrency and blockchain technologies can offer within their industries. In fact, some of the biggest names in global centralized systems, like Mark Zuckerberg (Facebook), Bill Gates (Microsoft) and Eric Schmidt (Google), have all indicated their interest and support for cryptocurrencies.

Lost jobs are inevitable

There is no question that the revolutionary technology behind bitcoin will have a tremendous impact on the global financial eco-system, and this will undoubtedly result in many people losing their jobs. This is one of the disadvantages that have emerged not only from the growth of cryptocurrency but in the creation of disruptive technologies as well.

Many companies in the payments, banking, and security industries will lose their value proposition if they do not adapt to emerging technologies. Once their profitability has been shaken, these companies will either lay off some employees or, even worse, close shop.

The introduction of cryptocurrency and its underlying technology to the financial services sector will have a similar effect to the introduction of robotics in the manufacturing industry. Many banks are already looking into how they can participate in the cryptocurrency scene with the hopes of remaining relevant in the ongoing financial revolution. The same banks are also known for scaling down their operations when their profitability is at stake.

Some jobs may become irrelevant but new jobs will also be created. When banks started using the internet, many bank employees were unfortunately laid off However, at the same time, new jobs were opened. In essence, jobs are evolving rather than merely disappearing.

4. Cryptocurrency as a new asset class

Gold has been traditionally known as the ultimate store of value because of its unique characteristics. Our bills and coins, or fiat currency, is more suitably called as a *medium of exchange* because of its transactional properties. These are also useful tools for regulation. Gold and currencies are two known asset classes or categories of investments.

With the increasing demand for cryptocurrencies notwithstanding the fixed supply, cryptocurrency prices have significantly increased and will continue to rise. Because of this, many individuals (retail) and institutional investors consider cryptocurrencies as a new type of investment.

Moreover, global fund managers and investment firms have recently created new cryptocurrency investment vehicles (options) which include actively managed crypto-asset hedge funds, futures, single cryptocurrency investment trusts, passive index funds, funds of funds, and dozens of applications for exchange-traded products.

More investments in cryptocurrencies

Investors have been continuously looking for better returns on their investments. Though they were initially hesitant to place their funds in cryptocurrencies, it became clear that cryptocurrencies have underlying value. Regardless of this underlying value, the dramatic rise in cryptocurrency prices has triggered the appetite of investors for managed cryptocurrency investments.

According to the Morgan Stanley Research, there are over 84 new 'crypto-funds' formed in 2017 with around $2 billion in capital. There were only 11 cryptocurrency investment funds in 2016. Another cryptocurrency investment tracker, HFR Cryptocurrency Index, estimates that the annual returns on the funds on the various cryptocurrency investment funds have averaged over 1,600%.

> If the demand for cryptocurrency continues to increase, experts foresee that the growth in the number and variety of investment options will continue at a significant pace.

Cryptocurrencies are here to stay. They solve real-world economic and technological challenges. In this chapter, we have emphasized the currency or transactional function of cryptocurrencies. Many cryptocurrencies, however, are not only used as currency. In a later chapter, we will go over some of the major cryptocurrencies and their powerful features.

Cryptocurrency compared with gold and fiat currency

	Traits of Currency	Gold	Fiat currency	Crypto-currency
Traditional traits	Is it interchangeable?	Yes	Yes	Yes
	Is it non-consumable (does not spoil)?	Yes	Yes	Yes
	Is it portable?	No	Yes	Yes
	Is it highly durable?	Yes	No	Yes
	Is it highly divisible (more than 2 decimal places)?	No	No	Yes
	Is it difficult to counterfeit?	No	No	Yes
	Is it easily *transactable*?	No	Yes	Yes
	Is it scarce?	Yes	No	Yes
New traits	Is the issuance or creation independent from a government?	Yes	No	Yes
	Is it decentralized?	No	No	**Yes**
	Is it programmable?	No	No	Yes

The table above shows the degree to which gold, fiat currency, and cryptocurrency meet the traditional traits of currency as well as the new traits made possible by the invention of cryptocurrency.

How can ordinary citizens benefit from cryptocurrency?

Regardless of financial and academic background, cryptocurrencies can help unbanked people connect to an international monetary system without the need for centralized authorities. The current financial system only allows well-off individuals to participate in a global financial market where opportunities are abundant.

Retail investors can have easy access to better paying financial instruments that could help them grow and manage their wealth better without going through a bank. Peer-to-peer loans, with highly competitive interest rates, can also be obtained without a tedious credit investigation process. Small business owners can quickly sell their products online and get paid immediately without the hefty processing charges. Cryptocurrency platforms can enable farmers in developing countries to obtain micro-insurance so they can still have food on the table in times of severe drought or flood.

Millions of individuals can enjoy the services of a traditional bank with the use of their mobile phones and basic access to mobile internet. Cryptocurrencies have been created not for the rich, who have access to the best fund managers, but for those who do not have access to such services.

Governments around the world are also looking into improving the delivery of public service by using cryptocurrency technology. Some governments have started implementing blockchain technology in healthcare data management, national identity management systems, tax and internal revenue monitoring, voting, and secure banking services.

The technology behind cryptocurrency can ensure a more transparent government which can improve efficiency and accountability.

Many cryptocurrencies currently offer various functionalities, and more will be invented as thousands of developers explore the possibilities of using the technology behind cryptocurrencies in solving multiple global challenges that can benefit a significant number of people. The financial and technological revolution has just begun.

It is thus crucial for governments to provide a healthy environment where young developers and entrepreneurs can explore the uses of cryptocurrencies.

In the next chapter, we will explore the first cryptocurrency and the technology behind it.

Key Points

1. Cryptocurrency offers a solution to economic challenges posed by the use of fiat currency.
2. The technology used in cryptocurrency can replace trust in human organizations.
3. There are compelling reasons why cryptocurrency can be used as a medium of exchange just like bills and coins.
4. The invention of cryptocurrencies is a disruptive force in our world.
5. A significant number of people can benefit from cryptocurrency and its underlying technology.

This page is intentionally left blank.

Chapter 3

BITCOIN DEMYSTIFIED

"I think the internet is going to be one of the major forces for reducing the role of government. The one thing that's missing but that will soon be developed is a reliable e-cash."

– Prof. Milton Friedman, American Economist, and Nobel Laureate

---

Note: This chapter contains a few highly-technical discussions. As much as I want to simplify the discussions, it is essential for you to understand the core technical aspects of bitcoin. You may want to reread this chapter a few times to fully appreciate the disruptive nature of bitcoin's underlying technology.

Bitcoin defined, distinguished

Bitcoin is the first commercially successful cryptocurrency. However, it is not merely the equivalent of *digital currency*.

A *digital currency* is similar to what banks currently use. It is a currency in electronic form, traded, exchanged, and eventually settled and reconciled at the end of the day.

What differentiates bitcoin from digital currency is the fact that it is decentralized. Bitcoin, just like any other cryptocurrency, is not issued by any government. The bitcoin network is maintained by *peers* – individuals and groups who collectively maintain the network without anyone having control over how the network will operate. It is a digital currency that works even without a central bank or a system administrator.

Digital currencies, like the dollars and euro you use when transacting online, remain highly centralized. This centralization depends on authorities to reconcile various independently-maintained records.

On the other hand, decentralized consensus used in bitcoin enables peers to agree on which transactions are valid. The consensus rules, which is made possible by computer codes, remove the need for reconciliation, ensuring that only legitimate transactions are included in the public ledger.

Bitcoin is also *permission-less*. You do not need the permission of any authority to be part of the network. Anyone can be a part of the network regardless of his or her background. Unlike centralized systems, where you need to have the proper 'credentials' to be part of the group, the bitcoin network does not discriminate. This makes bitcoin *neutral*.

Neutrality is crucial in a free market. Bitcoin is not linked to a government or institution making it possible for users to have complete control over their wealth. Bitcoin cannot be seized or devalued on a whim.

Another difference between bitcoin and digital currency is that *cryptography* is built in bitcoin (refer to Chapter 2) which means that the bitcoin network is inherently secure, with a low possibility of hacking and counterfeiting. The introduction of cryptography is one of the revolutionary components of bitcoin's underlying technology. Banks and other financial institutions need to install and maintain third-party security systems and processes to protect their databases which contain the transactions and balances of their clients' accounts.

Therefore, bitcoin is not simply a subset of digital currency. It is a revolutionary technology aimed to solve an economic problem.

Bitcoin as a currency

Perhaps, the most well-known use of bitcoin is as a medium of exchange.

In the first chapter, we defined what currency is and differentiated it with money. Though currency shares similar traits with money, such as being a medium of exchange and unit of account, it cannot be a store of value because it is simply backed by trust in the government and not by actual gold.

Bitcoin was envisioned as an electronic payment system – as a form of currency. In fact, Satoshi Nakamoto introduced bitcoin as a "**peer-to-peer electronic cash system**" back in 2008. It was primarily used to electronically transfer value from one person to another. Bitcoin was supposed to be an inflation-proof digital currency.

However, in recent months, many analysts agree that bitcoin may no longer be a currency but rather a new *asset class*. As an asset class, bitcoin is often called the *digital gold*. This term implies that bitcoin is more of a store of value rather than as a medium of exchange.

Why bitcoin is not the same as currency

In order for bitcoin to become a real currency, it should be easily used like bills and coins. There are three reasons why some experts say that bitcoin is not an effective medium of exchange.

First, there is a transaction fee and the transaction fee can be quite high and volatile. When the demand for bitcoin was limited to early adopters, transaction fees and its dollar equivalent were relatively low compared to traditional remittance fees. However, due to the significant increase in transactions, the limited scale of the bitcoin network compounded by the increase in the dollar value of bitcoin, bitcoin transaction fees became expensive especially for low-value transactions. Towards the end of 2017, transaction fees ranged from $25 to $35 when the bitcoin network was congested. There were times when fees go low as $10 if the network was uncongested. These amounts may further increase if the value of bitcoin against the US dollar rises. The fees, however, have normalized recently and now range from $0.10 to $3.

Second, the transaction confirmation time is becoming longer because of the sheer volume of transactions in the bitcoin blockchain. A typical bitcoin transaction is confirmed within a few minutes to less than an hour. Since only a limited number of transactions can be confirmed at a given point in time (every 10 minutes), a sudden surge in bitcoin transactions can create a *bottleneck*. This can cause delays in the confirmation process and also increases transaction fees since other people who want their transactions to be confirmed faster would be willing to pay higher fees.

The last reason is bitcoins' limited public adoption. Most of the merchants who make use of bitcoins are online. For bitcoin to become a real currency, it must have a massive adoption that even street vendors will accept bitcoins using their mobile phones. However, this is improbable in the near future.

These three major reasons make bitcoin less of a currency. However, it does not mean that bitcoin has lost its value since it is now considered as a better store of value than gold. We will discuss how bitcoin derives its value in the next chapter.

Bitcoin as a technology

Many people view bitcoin as a technological revolution rather than as a financial innovation. Andreas Antonopoulos, a well-known bitcoin authority and programmer, has defined bitcoin as "**a collection of concepts and technologies that form the basis of a digital ecosystem.**"

This definition highlights bitcoin as an enabling force for a truly digital economy. It emphasizes the fact that bitcoin is *not just a currency*, but rather an accumulation of various computer techniques that can bring digital commerce to a higher level.

The invention of bitcoin introduced a new wave of technological advancement that consists of the following:

-    A new way to communicate with other computers using a peer-to-peer (P2P) network (**the bitcoin protocol**)

- A public transaction record (**the blockchain**)
- A system of rules to create new units of currency and validate transactions (**consensus rules**)
- An algorithm that enables validation of transactions (**proof-of-work algorithm**)

Imagine building a house. You start with the house's foundation. Then, slowly add blocks that will support the structure. Building the house requires a preconceived plan, a *blueprint*, created by a team of architects and engineers. To implement the plan, carpenters, and other workers are required to transform the plan into reality. Eventually, when the house is finished, the owner can move in, use the house, and possibly make renovations.

Creating a cryptocurrency involves several participants. You have the team that created the cryptocurrency, and who wrote down their plans (roadmap) in a document called *whitepaper*. The *whitepaper* defines the problems solved by the cryptocurrency and how the creators propose to solve those problems. When the foundation for the blockchain has been established, users can start exploring the project and send transactions using the network.

Then, a community of volunteer workers helps in building the crypto-currency project. Some of these workers assist in validating transactions within the network. These workers are called *miners* and are rewarded units of the blockchain's cryptocurrency.

In this section, we will explore how the various components of the technology and the actors in the network interact to build the robust bitcoin ecosystem.

The Bitcoin Protocol

In computer science, a *protocol* is defined as "a set of rules governing the exchange or transmission of data between devices." In simple terms, it is a predefined language which is similar to a language we use in daily communication (e.g., English). To illustrate, a sender (Computer 1) will speak in English to a recipient (Computer 2) who understands English. Since the sender knows that the recipient understands English, the message is properly sent and well-received. In the illustration, English is the *protocol*, which acts as the medium of communication.

One of the most common protocols used by computers to communicate in the World Wide Web is the *hypertext transfer protocol* or HTTP. This is the text followed by "://" that usually precedes the name of a website. A more secure version is the HTTPS, wherein the letter "S" means *secured*. Internet browsers such as Google Chrome, Mozilla Firefox and Opera, use the HTTP protocol to send and receive files from the internet.

Similarly, the *bitcoin protocol* enables bitcoin wallets and other apps to connect to the bitcoin network. The bitcoin protocol makes it possible for peers to connect to the network without connecting to a central 'server' and obtaining permission to connect.

Much like a language's spelling, sentence composition, conventions, and grammar, the *bitcoin protocol* is composed of cryptography rules, common standards, common structures, message types, scripting, and other rules that define how applications can communicate within the network. These sets of rules make it possible for developers to develop applications that can connect to the bitcoin network and interact with other applications created by other developers.

Since it is a network, the easiest way to implement the *bitcoin protocol* is over the internet. Thus, bitcoin users can communicate with other users using the bitcoin protocol via the internet. The protocol can be run on a wide range of computing devices, including desktops, laptops, and smartphones.

Aside from its device flexibility, the *bitcoin protocol* has been developed *open-source*, which means the protocol is publicly available for anyone interested in validating, modifying, and redistributing the software code. Open-source software is often considered more secure than privately developed software because the public can help detect "bugs" or errors within the software's source code. Usually, open-source software has a more robust community which allows members to explore and to develop the software's functionality.

The *bitcoin protocol* makes bitcoin application development easily accessible to developers who can eventually support the growth of a healthy community of users. The open-source nature of the *bitcoin protocol* has also resulted to numerous cryptocurrencies. Some of the significant cryptocurrencies born after bitcoin will be discussed in the next chapter.

The Blockchain

When talking about the technology behind bitcoin, one cannot avoid discussing the *blockchain* – the revolutionary innovation that has propelled the advancement of cryptocurrency.

The heart of the cryptocurrency network is the *blockchain*. So what is the *blockchain*, and how does it work?

In the following short story, I will try to illustrate how the blockchain works using simple terms.

The Story of the Blockchain Community

Ana and Bob are members of a small, thriving island community. Ana recently borrowed money from Bob, and a promissory note signed by Ana proves this.

On the due date, Ana denied that she has an existing loan from Bob. She claimed that Bob forged the promissory note. Suddenly, Bob had to defend himself and prove that he did not forge Ana's signature. In the end, Bob was not able to collect from Ana.

To prevent parties from refusing to recognize valid private agreements, their leader, Connie decreed that all loan transactions between all parties should be recorded in a notebook called *registry of loans*. Every time a villager borrows from another villager, both parties have to go to the town hall where the registry is kept and ask the custodian to record their loan transaction.

*The issue between Ana and Bob illustrates the problem with **private agreements** and how it can be solved by a **central authority**. In this case, the central authority is Connie. Furthermore, the registry of loans is an example of a **centralized database**.*

A few years later, when the registry was almost full, a fire engulfed the town hall. The registry was burned. Many debtors denied their loan obligations after they heard that the registry was burned.

The destruction of the registry caused serious concerns in the community, and Connie had to quickly come up with a solution. Connie suggested maintaining multiple registries for loans. She gathered trusted members of the community, and gave each of them a notebook to write all loan transactions between community members. She called the appointed members as *Custodians of the Registry*.

Every time there is a loan transaction between two people, all of the custodians have to appear in the newly-constructed town hall and record the details of each loan transaction in their notebooks. This system ensures that even if multiple registries are destroyed, the transactions remain recorded and cannot be denied.

*The destruction of the registry illustrates the problem with centralized databases – there is a single point of failure. This problem has been solved by Connie when she distributed the records. The centralized database has been replaced by a **distributed database**, and the multiple registries (notebooks) represent the **multiple nodes**.*

The system worked for quite some time. However, in a strange order, Connie asked all the custodians to delete all the records relating to an individual, named Don, who had multiple loans from members of the community. Due to Connie's order, Don suddenly became free from his debts.

When the people of the community came to learn about what Connie did, they unanimously decided to exile her, along with Don, from the island.

Due to Connie's abuse of power, all the members of the community decided to keep a copy of the registry of loans. Every time a loan transaction is made between members of the community, all of them have to appear in the town hall and update their registries. They also agreed never to remove or delete any transaction already recorded in the registry.

*The problem with distributed databases is that they can remain centralized. A single authority can still exercise control over all the distributed nodes (registries) and can make changes as they deem fit. When members of the community lost trust in their leader, they decided to make the records **public** and to distribute the task of keeping the records to all members of the community. This system resulted in the loss of centralized control which is called **decentralization**.*

*Moreover, the agreement to never remove or delete any transaction resulted in **immutability** (unchangeability) of records which also made the registry **permanent**.*

Several years have passed, and the system was able to protect both debtors and creditors. However, an enterprising group of community members decided to create a fraudulent transaction by using a complicated scheme. They almost succeeded in creating the fraudulent loan, but many people eventually noticed that the transaction was incorrect.

The rest of the community refused to record the transaction in their registries which effectively made the fake transaction void. Furthermore, they decided to punish the enterprising group and banished them from the island.

Ever since the group was banished from the island, several individuals connived to try and manipulate the community's recording system but all of them failed.

Before a transaction is recorded in the registries, the community members check the validity of the transaction to be recorded. When a transaction is incorrect, they will not record it in their registries. For a transaction to be added, a majority of the community members should agree that such transaction is valid. This is how **consensus** *is formed, and voting is done to decide the validity of a transaction in the blockchain.*

As time passed, more notebooks were filled out. Every time a new notebook (registry) is used, it is always referenced to the previous notebook. The old notebooks were eventually stored in weather-proof, box-like containers called *blocks*. When full, these *blocks* are secured by locks and metal *chains* to ensure that they cannot be easily opened and modified.

After seeing how the community members organized their registries, one of the elders, who saw how the community's record-keeping system has evolved suggested calling the system as the *blockchain* – a collection of fully-replicated, decentralized, and immutable book of records.

This ends the story of the Blockchain Community.

We define the blockchain as a digital, decentralized, public ledger (record) of all transactions in the network. Transactions are grouped into *blocks* which are chronologically added and linked to a *chain* of records. This chain of records stores all the transactions that occurred in the network since the inception of the cryptocurrency. The same copy of the blockchain is maintained and updated by many users of the network. This system allows users of the network to keep track of their transactions without a system administrator or server.

Here is a breakdown of what the blockchain is:

- **It is a type of record-keeping system maintained in an online database.** It is similar to an accounting book or ledger kept in a computer. In our example earlier, this is the public registry.
- **Transactions are recorded in units called blocks.** Think of these blocks as pages in the public ledger. Each block in the ledger is referenced to the previous block.

- **It is public.** Anyone can view and verify the transactions recorded in the ledger.
- **It is decentralized.** No centralized server or authority controls the database.

The information in a block is ordered logically and chronologically. Each new block in the blockchain is cryptographically-linked to the previous block. Since cryptography is used, it will be difficult to change any data in the blockchain. This is because an attacker has to spend so much time and computing resources to decipher the unique key to unlock the link (reference) for each block.

The higher the *block height*, the more computing resources is required to change information on the block. The block height refers to the number of blocks in the chain between the most recent block and the first or *genesis block*. The block height of the *genesis block* is zero. The *genesis block* was mined by Satoshi Nakamoto.

Furthermore, the *consensus* from the network is required every time a block is added in the blockchain. A new block can only be added and recorded by network participants maintaining *full nodes* when it has been validated and verified by special network participants called *miners*. A *miner* validates transactions and creates blocks in the blockchain which the *full nodes* keep.

A *full node* downloads and maintains a complete copy of the blockchain. The blockchain copy maintained by *full nodes* is used to verify transactions in the network. A network participant who wishes to become a bitcoin *full node* is currently required to have at least 140 gigabytes of hard drive space.

These intricacies make blockchain challenging to understand but it keeps the network secure from bad participants.

Why trust the blockchain's security?
Many people argue that existing centralized database systems are more efficient and secure compared to the blockchain. However, there are

some serious concerns with centralized databases as discussed in the previous chapter. Primarily, centralized databases have a single point of attack and rely on access control to protect the system. This means that an attacker can solely focus on one location to compromise the entire system. Relying on access control is also a major problem since one can quickly gain control by imitating or corrupting anyone who has access to the database.

Blockchain technology has offered a solution to these problems making it more secure than traditional database systems. What, then, makes the blockchain more secure?

a. **Use of Cryptography.** Every block transaction in the blockchain is time-stamped and chronologically-linked (referenced) to the previous block. The link is made secure by cryptography. This means that a transaction in a block cannot be changed without modifying all the cryptographically and chronologically-linked blocks. Modifying all linked blocks is nearly impossible which makes transactions recorded in the blockchain secure and permanent.

b. **Decentralization.** A copy of the bitcoin blockchain is distributed among peers across different computers. As discussed earlier, no single authority controls the network. Instead, independent peers in the network help in validating transactions, without going through an intermediary. Such process makes validating transactions quicker and less expensive.

The Rules of Bitcoin and Consensus

Bitcoin was the first successful cryptocurrency. Since the internet was invented, many people have tried to introduce the concept of "e-money" but all have failed... until bitcoin was created in 2008.

One of the significant challenges that bitcoin's predecessors faced is the danger of *digital counterfeiting*. As we all know, anything uploaded on the internet can be reproduced quickly with minimal cost. This is why cryptography, consensus rules, and proof-of-work (POW) were adopted in bitcoin.

Bitcoin consensus rules are the specific set of rules that full nodes will consistently enforce to validate and record transaction blocks. It is called *consensus rules* because the full nodes must form a consensus or agreement before the implementation of a new rule. Experts often refer to the bitcoin consensus rules as *rules of bitcoin*.

Think about *consensus rules* as the rules for basketball, and the full nodes as the game scorers who keep track of the records of the game. When a player successfully makes a basket, the team scores two points, and the ball goes to the other side. You cannot have more than two points per basket, unless it is made outside of the three-point arc. If the scorers notice that the referee awarded three points to a two-point basket, the scorers will ignore the extra point or invalidate the points awarded.

Bitcoin consensus rules also prohibit certain acts that do not conform to standard just like the fouls and violations in basketball. Rules need to be enforced to avoid bad players from manipulating the system, and creating fake transactions (counterfeiting). For example, the bitcoin consensus rules require that transaction blocks must be in the correct data format and that miners who successfully validated a block, are only rewarded a certain number of bitcoins (currently, 12.5 bitcoins). If a miner generated a block that contains more bitcoins than what is allowed, *full nodes* (scorers) will reject recording the block. The consensus rules make counterfeiting even more difficult since the counterfeiter has to consider the rules when introducing fraudulent transactions in the network. A counterfeiter would have to convince full nodes to accept the fake transaction. Otherwise, the fake transactions will just be overlooked, and will never be recorded, rendering these transactions void.

Being a highly-participatory network, bitcoin participants can propose *adding* new consensus rules. This can generally be done through a *soft fork* while *removing* any consensus rule requires a *hard fork*. If the bitcoin network disagrees about the consensus rules, then the network splits into two or more independent pieces.

There have been a few bitcoin *splits* in recent years. The earliest bitcoin split was *litecoin* in 2011 and subsequently followed by *bitcoin cash* (BCH) and *bitcoin gold* (BTG) both in 2017. When splits resulting from a hard fork occur, the new cryptocurrency will have its own blockchain but will have the same blockchain as bitcoin until the point of split. Bitcoin holders often receive an equivalent number of the new cryptocurrency just like what happened with *bitcoin cash* and *bitcoin gold*.

Who controls the bitcoin network?

Knowing that bitcoin has no central authority over the network can be difficult to understand. This is because we grew up in a *trust-based economy* where we have to trust institutions, like governments and banks, to survive. It is thus essential to understand that control rests not on a few parties but with the network of peers. This is called *consensus*.

The bitcoin network is not owned or controlled by anyone just like the technology behind email. Although a team of volunteer developers continues to improve the bitcoin software, they cannot just make changes in the bitcoin protocol and rules without the consensus of all users.

In bitcoin, *consensus* means "no significant objection among the set of *people who 'matter.'*" In the bitcoin network, *people who matter* are the miners who validate transactions. Miners matter because they have invested a significant amount of resources to validate transactions. The requirement to dedicate significant computing resources also prevents anyone from creating fake voters and manipulating the "election" to arrive at a consensus. This system makes manipulating the consensus expensive.

The consensus of nearly all, if not all, of the users is the standard requirement to implement a hard fork. This means that there should be no significant number of miners who will actively oppose the hard fork. For clarity, this level of agreement is called non-*contentious* or *near-unanimous consensus*.

Technical discussions on how to improve bitcoin's software, which are usually embodied in documents called *bitcoin improvement proposals* (BIP), do not require non-contentious or near-unanimous consensus. BIPs only require *general agreement* which means "a strong majority when the participants are weighted for expertise and/or strength of argument." For example, if four experts strongly agree to something and provide persuasive arguments for it but five laymen (non-experts) merely state that they oppose the proposal, then the proposal has consensus. However, if four experts present strong arguments for a proposal, and three experts present equally strong arguments against it, then it can be said that the proposal has no consensus.

A *consensus* is a way for the network to resolve issues and upgrade the network without any single authority making decisions. This makes the bitcoin network genuinely decentralized.

Proof-of-Work and Mining

In the earlier illustration using basketball, we talked about the scorers or network participants maintaining full nodes, and the referees or the miners.

Full nodes are computers that maintain a complete copy of the blockchain. Before they *record* new blocks in the blockchain, they have to verify the validity of the block. However, who creates the blocks?

To answer this question, let's briefly go over how a bitcoin transaction works.

How bitcoin transaction works

Assume Eric wants to transfer 0.01 bitcoin to Felly. Eric has previously received a bitcoin from his friend Gem. The bitcoin that Eric received from Gem is currently stored in his bitcoin wallet. The bitcoin wallet is an app on his mobile phone that stores the *digital keys* to Eric's bitcoins (more on this topic in Chapter 5).

Eric logs into his bitcoin wallet and clicks on "Send Bitcoin." He is prompted to input the recipient's bitcoin address and the amount of bitcoin he is sending. After completing all the required information, he is asked to pay a "transaction fee" of 0.001. Eric clicks "Send." He reviews the transaction, and clicks "Confirm." The confirmation ends Eric's interactions with the phone app, but this begins the app's interaction with the bitcoin network.

The bitcoin wallet app then "signs" the transaction with Eric's *digital signature*. The digital signature has been created when Eric opened an account with the bitcoin wallet app. Within seconds after confirmation, the transaction is broadcasted to the bitcoin network and added to the *unconfirmed transactions* pool known as *mempool*. Once broadcasted, Felly's bitcoin wallet app will wait for the transaction to be confirmed.

Eric's digitally-signed 'send' transaction is subsequently picked up from the *mempool* by miners who will verify the validity of the transaction by checking Eric's digital signature. Eric's transaction is subsequently compiled together with other people's transactions in a *candidate block*. Remember that a *block* is a collection of transactions. Imagine that a block is a box that contains pieces of paper with each piece containing transaction details from several network participants.

There will be several miners who will compete to try and win the right to include their candidate block to the blockchain. This competition involves computing for a complex mathematical puzzle which can be solved within 10 minutes. The first miner to present a solution to this puzzle within the given timeframe will have the right to add their candidate block into the blockchain and will be rewarded new bitcoins. The right to add the candidate block to the blockchain is called *proof-of-work*. The entire process of creating candidate blocks and competing to solve the mathematical puzzle is called *mining*.

A new block added on top of the block containing Eric's transaction counts as one *confirmation*. After a few confirmations (usually 2 to 6 confirmations), Felly's wallet will show an additional 0.01 bitcoin which she can use for other transactions.

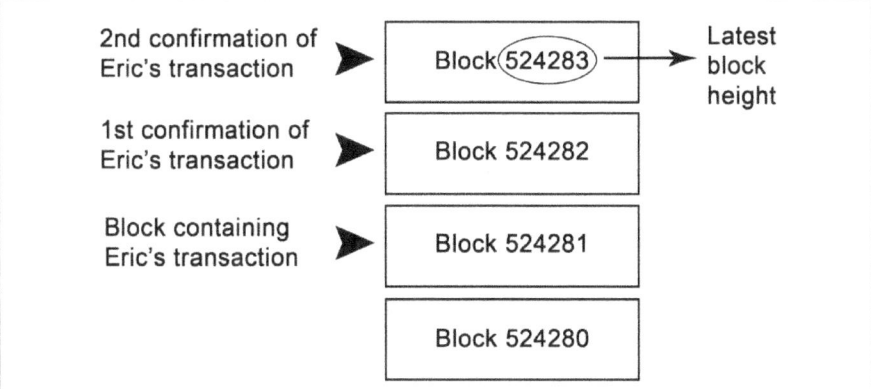

In summary, this is what happens behind the scenes:

- Eric's transactions were bundled together into a block;
- Miners verify the transactions within each block;
- Miners then solve a mathematical puzzle known as a *proof-of-work* problem;
- Freshly-created bitcoins are rewarded to the first miner who solves each block's problem; and
- Verified transactions are propagated in the network, and are stored in the public blockchain by full nodes.

One of the most critical mechanisms introduced by Satoshi Nakamoto, that makes the bitcoin network secure, is the *proof-of-work*. The proof-of-work concept was first adapted for financial transactions by game developer Hal Finney in 2004 which was later integrated by Satoshi in bitcoin. Hal Finney was also the recipient in the first-ever bitcoin transaction.

Investopedia defines *proof-of-work* as **"a system that requires a not-insignificant but feasible amount of effort in order to deter frivolous or malicious uses of computing power, such as sending spam emails or launching denial of service attacks."** In bitcoin, it is a process in the network that requires transactions to be validated by miners through solving computer or mathematical puzzles. Many other cryptocurrencies also use proof-of-work.

As discussed earlier, anyone can generate transactions and add blocks to the blockchain. *Proof-of-work* is a way of screening invalid blocks. Miners are required to validate transactions, create candidate blocks and then solve complex mathematical puzzles so that their candidate blocks can be included in the blockchain.

The mining software automatically checks if all the information in the transaction is valid before it is added to a candidate block. This validation process includes checking if the recipient has authority to spend the bitcoin that is attached to the transaction.

Proof-of-work can be imagined as the effort required in solving an enormous Sudoku puzzle with thousands of rows and columns. It is difficult to fill in all the boxes but it can be solved over a specific time frame.

A Sudoku puzzle also has a crucial feature – *asymmetry*. Asymmetry means that even if it is difficult to complete the puzzle, it is easy to verify if the answer is correct. Once a miner claims to complete a block, full nodes can quickly verify if the puzzle was correctly completed. Full nodes can reject candidate blocks that were not correctly generated.

The *proof-of-work's* difficulty is adjusted to limit the rate at which new blocks can be generated by the network to only one block roughly every 10 minutes. It is like adding a few thousands of rows and columns to the Sudoku puzzle. The difficulty required to solve the puzzle makes it impossible to predict which miner will be able to solve the puzzle and generate the new block on the blockchain. This makes mining more like a lottery than a race.

Securing the blockchain

Valid blocks are referenced to the previously-generated blocks using cryptography through a technique called *hashing*. In Chapter 1, we defined a *hash function* as a mathematical process that takes input data of any size, in this case, a reference to the previous block, then performs an operation on it, and returns output data of a fixed size called a *hash*.

A valid block contains the hash of the preceding block. This means that each new block is connected to a chain of blocks that together contain a significant amount of "work." Changing a block in the blockchain requires regenerating all the predecessors and successors as well as redoing the work they contain. This makes the blockchain difficult to hack and protects the blockchain from being tampered with.

Bitcoin uses the *SHA-256* (Secure Hashing Algorithm 256-bit) hash algorithm to generate verifiable "random" numbers in a way that requires a predictable amount of computing effort.

Bitcoin Lifecycle

SENDER

Using the bitcoin app / wallet:

- scans / copies recipient's bitcoin address
- inputs amount to be sent
- confirms transaction details and presses 'Send'

SENDER'S BITCOIN APP / WALLET

(Machine)

- digitally signs the transaction using sender's digital keys
- broadcasts the verified transaction to the bitcoin network

MINERS

- include the sender's transaction in their candidate blocks
- compete in solving the proof-of-work problem ("mining")

FULL NODES

- verify the results of the mining process
- add the verified block into their copy of the blockchain
- help in propagating the verified block

RECIPIENT'S BITCOIN APP / WALLET

- is notified of the first confirmation of the transaction
- waits for more confirmations as new blocks are added in the bitcoin network

* After a few more confirmations, the app will show that the recipient has received the bitcoin from the sender

END

Transaction fees

Another interesting security feature of the bitcoin blockchain is the imposition of *transaction fees*. Aside from compensating bitcoin miners for securing the network, transaction fees serve as a security mechanism by making it economically unviable for hackers to flood the network with spurious transactions.

Transaction fees, which are automatically calculated and included in the transaction by the bitcoin wallet, serve as an incentive to include a transaction into the next block. This also serves as a disincentive against attempts of abusing the system by adding a small cost on every transaction. The winning miner will be awarded the transaction fee accumulated for the block, together with new bitcoins.

How is the transaction fee computed?

The transaction fee is calculated based on the following:

- Size of the transaction in kilobytes (not the value of the transaction), and
- Market forces

Bitcoin miners prioritize transactions based on many criteria including the amount of transaction fee paid by the sender. Transaction fees thus affect how fast a transaction is processed. A transaction with a small or insufficient fee will most likely be delayed since it will be added in later blocks. Worse, it may not be processed at all. A transaction with sufficient transaction fee will most probably be picked up by miners from the mempool and immediately included in the next block.

In recent months, the transaction fees have fluctuated significantly due to the increased demand for bitcoin. Towards the end of 2017, the fee increased up to $40 per transaction. However, due to the sudden drop in demand for bitcoin in the first quarter of 2018, the fees returned to around $0.10 per transaction.

Bitcoin economics and the purpose of mining

Many people have misconceptions about the purpose of bitcoin *mining*. It is perceived primarily as the process of creating bitcoin. However, this is not its primary purpose.

Mining is the primary security feature of the entire bitcoin system. The creation and awarding of new bitcoins is merely the incentive for those who help secure transaction blocks using proof-of-work.

Bitcoin *mining* is done in order to secure the blockchain via proof-of-work as well as:

- To validate transactions sent to the network;
- To reward miners with new bitcoins and transaction fees for performing the previous task; and
- To implement bitcoin's monetary supply.

Bitcoin *mining* requires a lot of computing power provided by specialized hardware called *application-specific integrated circuits* (ASIC) and a special program. Miners will use this program and a lot of energy that runs the ASICs to compete with other miners to win the proof-of-work for the block. The winning miner attaches the proof-of-work to the block and earns the right to add it to the blockchain.

From a conceptual point of view, it is called *mining* because it follows the idea of diminishing returns which is similar to mining for gold and other precious metals. You may continue to invest in specialized equipment (ASIC) and spend more resources (electricity) to mine a decreasing supply of precious metals (bitcoins). You mine because you know the price of precious metals will continue to rise given its limited supply.

The maximum amount of newly-created bitcoin a miner can earn from a block decreases approximately every four years (or every 210,000 blocks). In the early years of bitcoin, miners earn 50 bitcoins per block. The reward was halved in November 2012, and it halved again to 12.5 bitcoins in July 2016. This follows bitcoin's monetary formula, wherein bitcoin mining rewards will decrease exponentially until the year 2140 when all bitcoins will have been issued. After the year 2140, no new bitcoins will be created. Consequently, miners will be rewarded solely through transaction fees. As of June 2018, there are around 17.1 million bitcoins in circulation.

The limited (finite) and diminishing issuance of bitcoin creates a fixed monetary supply that prevents currency devaluation and resists inflation (refer to Chapter 1).

The cost of mining bitcoins

During the early years of bitcoin, the first miners were just cryptography enthusiasts. These people were interested in the project and shared their spare computing power to validate transactions and secure the blockchain so that they could be rewarded with bitcoins. Back then, the computing power required to mine bitcoins was not too difficult that ordinary CPUs can successfully mine several bitcoins.

Bitcoins in circulation

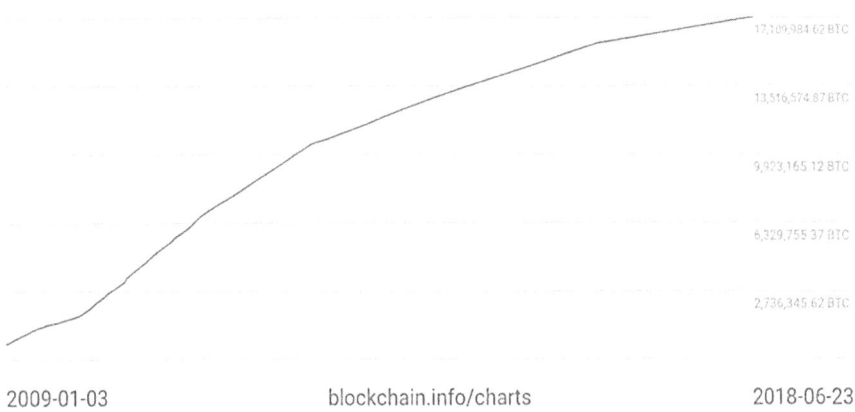

blockchain.info/charts

2009-01-03   2018-06-23

The total number of bitcoins that have already been mined as of June 23, 2018 is around 17.1 million.

As the bitcoin network expanded and the price of bitcoin dramatically increased, more people saw mining as a potential business. Miners began investing in warehouses and hardware to mine as many bitcoins as possible. However, because of the design of bitcoin's money supply, the mathematical puzzles that miners solve became more complex and required more computing power. The computing power needed to solve the complex mathematical problems can only be extracted from specialized equipment called *application-specific integrated circuit* (ASIC) that consumes staggering amounts of electricity to run 24/7. ASICs are made with the sole purpose of obtaining proof-of-work for its owner and cannot be repurposed for other uses.

Running ASICs does not come cheap. Thus, mining bitcoins today require significant investments in equipment and electricity. According to the Bitcoin Energy Consumption Index, the global energy usage of all bitcoin mining as of early 2018 is estimated to be equivalent to the power consumption of Denmark which has a population of 5.7 million. It is estimated that the electric consumption used for mining will eventually approach to that of Bangladesh – a place where 163 million people use electricity.

A research done by Elite Fixtures found that the cost of mining one bitcoin varies significantly around the world. From as little as $531 in Venezuela, where electricity is practically free due to government subsidy, up to a stunning $26,170 in South Korea where electricity is most expensive.

A mining farm of Genesis Mining located in Iceland. The picture shows mainly Zeus scrypt miners. Photo from Wikipedia

Mining Pools and Cloud Mining

For those who would still want to mine bitcoins given a limited budget, they could join mining pools. Instead of attempting to generate blocks alone, small miners can pool their resources to increase their chances of successfully winning proof-of-work for a block and share the earned reward. However, operating a mining pool still requires significant technical knowledge.

Mining pools began when the difficulty for mining increased to the point where it could take years for slower miners to successfully find proof-of-work for a block. By pooling their resources, the mining pool could generate blocks more quickly, and members of the pool could receive a portion of the block reward on a consistent basis, rather than randomly once every few years.

Cloud mining: legit or scam?

An emerging approach to passively investing in bitcoin is through *cloud mining*. *Cloud mining* is the process of buying hashing power from dedicated mining facilities operated by a reputable company who use their equipment to mine bitcoin and other cryptocurrencies. It is often marketed as renting hash power measured in gigahertz per second (GH/s).

Cloud mining companies claim that the main advantage of this method of bitcoin investing is that users neither need to have an in-depth knowledge of mining nor buy expensive mining equipment. Many of these companies are also manufacturers of ASICs or are partners with ASIC manufacturers. To save costs, cloud mining companies have placed their mining facilities in countries like Iceland and China where electricity is cheap.

Cloud mining makes sense since buyers or renters of hashing power will generate a profit if the price of bitcoin continues to rise. However, this also means that the buyer/renter bears the risk of loss if the price of bitcoin goes down.

There are a few legitimate cloud mining services that are available in the market. However, there has also been a proliferation of fake cloud mining companies that operate a Ponzi scheme. These Ponzi schemes systematically collect from referrals and not from actual mining operations. All Ponzi schemes eventually crumble, and a significant number of the "investors" lose money.

Perhaps a challenge for people who want to mine bitcoin through cloud mining is to vet the company that operates the facility properly. A responsible investor will take some time to research before investing in a cloud mining platform. If in doubt about the reputation of a cloud mining company, do not invest!

At the end of the day, limited home-based mining is no longer profitable. The average home miner will have to struggle to recover the cost of mining hardware and electricity.

The situation may improve in the future if ASIC mining hardware innovation reaches the point of diminishing returns. Coupled with cheaper electricity, mining bitcoin may once again become profitable for small individual miners around the world.

Until then, large mining companies and pools will dominate the bitcoin mining scene now and in the near future. People who want to dabble in bitcoins would find that buying bitcoin from an exchange is an easier way to own bitcoins.

Is proof-of-work wasteful?

Experts agree that bitcoin mining using proof-of-work is expensive. Bitcoin's growth and mining difficulty are exponentially tied to energy consumption, and critics see this as a significant issue under the proof-of-work model. Spending massive amounts of energy trying to solve a mathematical puzzle is often seen as wasteful. This has led other cryptocurrency developers to use other means of securing the blockchain. The predominantly cheaper alternative is called *proof-of-stake* (POS).

The idea behind *proof-of-stake* significantly varies from proof-of-work. Instead of creating blocks through competitive means, the blocks are generated based on the miner's ownership, or *stake*, in the currency. Under the *proof-of-stake* system, *forgers* (the equivalent of miners in proof-of-work) are chosen to generate blocks based on their stake in a currency and the age of that stake within the blockchain's network. Some of the cryptocurrencies that use proof-of-stake are *Cardano*, *OmiseGo*, *Qtum*, and *Ardor*.

The POS method of securing the blockchain solves the problem of costly electric consumption. This, however, creates a scenario wherein cryptocurrency holders would instead hoard the cryptocurrency than use them for transactions. Critics of this model claim that cryptocurrencies using *proof-of-stake* will become less of a currency and more of a long-term investment earning passive income.

If we look back at the intention of Satoshi Nakamoto when he created bitcoin, proof-of-work was primarily designed as an inherent security feature. Proof-of-work was integrated to prevent bad participants from manipulating the network by making it so expensive for any single entity to launch an attack against the network. The bitcoin blockchain now represents an accumulated amount of proof-of-work that it becomes impossible to break the chain and manipulate the network without incurring billions of dollars' worth of losses.

Thus, we can surmise that the energy spent to run the mining equipment is actually representative of the cost of securing the bitcoin network, a global peer-to-peer currency system that remains uncompromised since its inception. The bitcoin network is trustless, permissionless, and borderless.

Would you rather pay to fix a failed system or pay to make the system immune to hacking?

Key Points

In this chapter, we have extensively discussed the critical aspects of the amazing technology behind bitcoin.

The key takeaways from this chapter are:

1. Bitcoin is the first commercially viable cryptocurrency and remains to be the dominant cryptocurrency.
2. Bitcoin is powered by a unique set of technologies – the bitcoin protocol, the blockchain, consensus rules, and proof-of-work.
3. The bitcoin protocol enables computers to communicate with the bitcoin network. Consensus rules allow the growth of the bitcoin network without a central authority. Proof-of-work gives uncompromising security to the network. The blockchain enables the transparency and immutability of transaction records.
4. The blockchain is bitcoin's unique recordkeeping system that aggregates transactions by block.
5. Miners secure the bitcoin network and are rewarded with freshly-created bitcoins.

After learning about the technology behind bitcoin and its potential impact on our world, it is clear that bitcoin has an underlying value. In the next chapter, we will discuss the various issues surrounding the price of bitcoin.

Chapter 4

THE VALUE OF BITCOIN

"Economists and journalists often get caught up in this question: Why does Bitcoin have value? And the answer is very easy. Because it is useful and scarce."

– Erik Voorhees, CEO of ShapeShift.io and Co-founder of Coinapult

Tulip mania

In the 1630s, there was a frenzy for tulips. According to stories, almost everyone in the Netherlands was involved in trading tulips. Back then, the tulip was considered a rare flower valued for its unique beauty. Contracts called *tulip futures* were traded for up to 10 times the salary of a skilled craftsman. A *tulip futures* contract is a binding agreement to buy specific quantities of tulip bulbs at an identified price and to be delivered at a defined time in the future. No physical tulips were traded; only futures contracts to buy tulip bulbs at a determined price were being exchanged between investors. They say that the tulip mania reached a point where no one wanted to buy bulbs, and everyone was only interested in the profits.

At the height of the mania in 1636 to early 1637, tulip futures were sold for crazy prices equivalent to the cost of houses. However, in February 1637, the market prices abruptly crashed when buyers did not show up because of the plague. Bulbs started getting traded at a fraction of its inflated price, leaving many people in financial ruin. Accordingly, desperate bankrupts threw themselves in canals. The Dutch government eventually stepped in to manage the effects of the devastating market crash.

Although the veracity of this story has been put into question because of the lack of economic records during that time, the term *tulip mania* is now often used figuratively to refer to any large economic bubble when asset prices deviate from their underlying or intrinsic values. In fact, the *tulip mania* is known as one of the earliest recorded forms of an asset bubble.

The Dot-Com Bubble

During the last decade of the twentieth century, the Internet has been created. It helped usher in a new world order that made communication, commerce and living a lot easier. Back then, however, many believed that the internet was a scam and only geeks could use such technology.

It was soon proven that the internet was an amazing technology. People began investing in the stocks of companies that have websites on the internet or developing technologies that connect to the internet. Investors put in billions of dollars' worth of investment money on these Internet-based companies.

The staggering amount of money invested in 'dot-com' companies eventually created a *bubble*. A *bubble* is a fancy term used in the business world to refer to an economy driven by speculation without the creation of real value. It is called a *bubble* because asset prices are *inflated* or overpriced due to demand. Moreover, when the *bubble* pops, a domino effect will follow which starts with the assets losing significant value.

The *dot-com bubble* eventually burst in 2002. Many dot-com companies failed or lost market value. Billions of dollars were lost in just a year. A few companies, like *Amazon* and *eBay*, survived the market crash and eventually recovered to become some of the world's biggest companies. Jeff Bezos, Amazon's founder, is now the wealthiest person on earth, surpassing Microsoft's Bill Gates by a long shot!

A few years later, the information technology industry stabilized. Slowly, many companies that belong in this industry gained a considerable market share. These companies dominated the I.T. sector, which became a dominant segment of the world's economy.

Today, world economic and business leaders are sounding the alarm again for another great financial disaster. They say that it may become the most prominent *bubble* to ever burst in history. This new *bubble* is called *bitcoin*.

Recently, there was a slew of criticisms regarding bitcoin being the next big bubble. From JP Morgan Chase & Co.'s CEO, Jamie Dimon, to the world's third richest person and well-known stock investor, Warren Buffet, many big names in the world of finance have branded bitcoin as something to avoid "just like the plague" (Jack Bogle).

They argue that cryptocurrencies have no intrinsic value and should have a zero price tag simply because they are not backed by precious metals or governments. They usually imply that cryptocurrencies have been created out of thin air and are only driven by speculation.

In this chapter, we will attempt to unravel the issues about bitcoin valuation, and if bitcoin really is a *bubble*. We will also discuss how bitcoin and other cryptocurrencies can acquire value while exploring the key drivers that affect cryptocurrency prices.

Is bitcoin a bubble waiting to burst?

The dramatic rise in the price of bitcoin in the past few years has led many experts to brand bitcoin as the "tulip mania 2.0" or the next "dot-com bubble."

What is a bubble?

It is important to understand what a *bubble* is to form an opinion whether bitcoin is a *bubble* or not.

Investopedia defines a *bubble* as an "economic cycle characterized by a rapid escalation of asset prices followed by a contraction." Such a price drop is known as a *crash* or a *bubble burst* which is created by a surge in asset prices without economic or positive fundamental basis and is driven by enthusiastic market behavior. Eventually, it will reach a point where no investors are willing to buy at the elevated price which will result in a massive sell-off and cause the bubble to *deflate*.

It is important to note that *bubbles* can only be confirmed after it happens.

Characteristics of a bubble

The best thing to do to identify a *bubble* is by looking into prevailing conditions that indicate the possibility of a *bubble* brewing. Some of the characteristics of a potential *bubble* are the following:

1. Borrowing money to purchase or "invest" (leveraging);
2. Lending to high-risk individuals (people who might not be able to pay);
3. Borrowing or lending money based on the prospect of the asset's future price rather than based on the ability of the borrower to pay;
4. Lending money based on the value of the collateral rather than the risk of non-payment;
5. Increased media mileage or coverage relating to the asset;
6. A significant infusion of funds into the asset resulting to demand-supply imbalance (significantly more buyers); and
7. Low-interest rates for borrowing which encourage lending and borrowing

Bitcoin bubble deflating

Based on the list above, the current environment for bitcoin is descriptive of an impending short-term bubble burst. With the recent price slump, some may even argue that the bitcoin bubble has already deflated. Prices of bitcoin dropped from near $20,000 in December 2017 to around $7,000 in early April 2018. This 60-percent price drop happened in less than four months.

Many stories in social media have been shared numerous times describing the financial ruin brought about by the sudden drop in bitcoin's price. These people have fallen to the FOMO ("fear of missing out") trap, selling their properties, and borrowing money to buy bitcoin at the peak of its prices without adequately understanding the risks of investing in bitcoin. They soon became stuck when the prices started plunging. Eventually, these people sold their holdings at significant losses.

If the bitcoin bubble did burst or deflate, the questions to be asked now are: **Will the price of bitcoin ever recover? Or will it continue to drop?** These questions are quite tricky to answer but these could be best explained by looking into whether bitcoin has an underlying value. If bitcoin has an underlying value, perhaps the downward price movement may be temporary.

Phases of a Traditional Asset Bubble

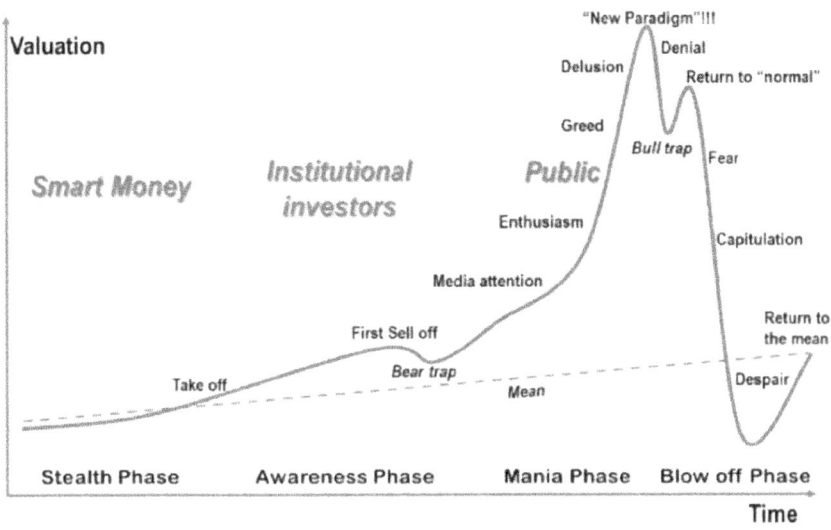

The graph above shows the four phases of a traditional asset bubble – stealth, awareness, mania and blow-off. Since institutional investors have only recently started investing in bitcoin, many experts believe that bitcoin may still be in the early stage of the awareness phase. Source: Dr. Jean-Paul Rodrigue (Hofstra University)

The intrinsic value of bitcoin

Many economists have criticized cryptocurrencies as having no *intrinsic value*. What does *intrinsic value* mean?

Investopedia defines *intrinsic value* as "the *actual value* of a company or an asset based on an underlying perception of its true value including all aspects of the business, in terms of both tangible and intangible factors." A stock's *intrinsic value* then lies on the company's business model (qualitative) and current and future financial performance (quantitative). For gold, its unique physical attributes primarily define its value.

In the context of cryptocurrency, *intrinsic value* refers to the perceived worth of a cryptocurrency based on its *future utility*. Since there are no companies running most cryptocurrencies, no historical financial statements can be used to assess the price growth of the cryptocurrencies.

Will the cryptocurrency solve an underlying problem? Will people pay to use the cryptocurrency's platform? In bitcoin's case, will it really become a sustainable store of value? These are some of the questions to be asked when evaluating the intrinsic value of cryptocurrencies.

It is therefore difficult to identify bitcoin's intrinsic value since there is no company behind it, and it has no physical attributes. However, the absence of these features may provide a basis for bitcoin's intrinsic value.

Without any company and physical form, bitcoin is still able to function as the first global decentralized digital asset which can be used and stored without the interference of government or banks.

Furthermore, bitcoin's scarcity and resistance to inflation makes it even more comparable to gold. In our digital world today, there are no other assets that can be a better tool for storing and exchanging value.

Gold versus bitcoin

There is an ongoing debate as to which asset people would use as a store of value – gold or bitcoin? On the one hand, there is gold which has been historically used as the ultimate store of value. Its current market capitalization and liquidity is proof of its dominance.

Then, there is bitcoin. A relatively young asset class that has been created in today's highly-digital world. It has considerably low trading volume compared to gold, but it also has unique attributes that resulted in it being called the *digital gold*.

Clearly, bitcoin will continue to gain popularity as a store of value, especially among the young populace who may want to hold value in digital form without the use of third parties – features that gold does not possess.

In the end, bitcoin's intrinsic value shall be driven primarily by people who will prefer bitcoin over gold as a store of value and medium of exchange.

Valuing bitcoin

It is clear that bitcoin does have some value. However, the challenge now is finding the right price for bitcoin.

There is no single way to value or price bitcoin and other cryptocurrencies because these are relatively new creations. There are no expected future cash flows or income, and there is no entity behind bitcoin that can be evaluated for past performance (like financial statements).

Hence, various experts from the field of investing, technology, and economics have come up with different models in an attempt to value bitcoin. To simplify, we have limited our discussion on bitcoin's valuation (or pricing) based on the following schools of thought:

1. As an asset (commodity),
2. As a network technology, and
3. As a currency (money system).

Key Assumptions

Keep in mind that each school of thought for valuing bitcoin will have different assumptions. There are two critical assumptions in the following valuation methods that will be discussed: first, interest in bitcoin will continue to grow; and second, the supply of bitcoin will approach 21 million as specified in the original schedule. All of those bitcoins will have been mined by the year 2140. Currently, there are around 17 million bitcoins in circulation.

Bitcoin Charts

The graph above shows the price history of bitcoin from June 18, 2017 to June 18, 2018. In December 2017, the market capitalization of bitcoin exceeded $320 billion, and the price per bitcoin reached $20,000. Screenshot from coinmarketcap.com

Valuing bitcoin as an asset

Gold, known as the ultimate store of value, is often compared to bitcoin primarily because of its utility, durability (not consumable), and predictable supply. As discussed in the previous chapter, the scarcity of bitcoin makes it inflation-proof. These are the reasons why some optimistic analysts call bitcoin as the *digital gold* implying that it is the preferred store of value for the younger and future generations.

Every day, more and more investors consider bitcoin as a new asset class. Today, the global community of investors has a better understanding that cryptocurrencies will not just vanish out of thin air one day. However, it is still difficult to assess the fundamental or underlying value of *crypto-assets*.

If bitcoin is considered as a new asset class, one way to determine its value is to compare it to the total value of gold reserves. The estimated total value of gold that has been mined is around $8 trillion. The current market capitalization or total market value of bitcoin is around $200 billion or 2.5 percent of the total value of gold as of March 2018.

Assuming that bitcoin will eventually capture 10 percent of gold's total market cap, bitcoin's market cap can reach up to $800 billion which will result in an estimated price of $38,000 per bitcoin. This method, of course, is a simplistic approach to valuation since there are many factors to be considered such as global demand and supply, regulation, and long-term utility.

Valuing bitcoin as a network technology

As a network-based technology, bitcoin's rise is often compared to the growth of social networking sites like *Facebook* and *Twitter*.

Fundstrat's Tom Lee, a leading bitcoin analyst and investor, uses the concept of *network effect* and *Metcalfe's Law* to explain the value of bitcoin. According to these valuation theories, the more engagement the network has, the more value gets created.

Metcalfe's Law

Robert Metcalfe, one of the inventors of Ethernet, proposed a formula in the 1980s that describes the value of a telecommunications network as proportional to the square of the number of connected users of the system (n^2). This formula eventually became known as *Metcalfe's Law* (M).

$$M = n^2$$

The formula has stood the test of time and became prominent for studying network effects and valuing online networks. In fact, the revenues (a key indicator for value) of social networking sites, such as *Facebook* and its Chinese equivalent *Tencent*, were found out to be proportional to the square of the sites' monthly active users (the Metcalfe's formula).

Using Metcalfe's Law also resulted to a near-perfect correlation with bitcoin's, and even ethereum's, dollar price. Analysts thus suggest that bitcoin and other cryptocurrencies that have reached critical user base behave similarly to online social networks such as *Facebook* with their value defined by their usage. In bitcoin's case, usage can be measured by daily transactions and the number of unique active bitcoin addresses.

Lee and other bitcoin analysts cautioned investors that using this valuation model in the short-term may not be a wise move. Instead, they suggested that the model be used to value bitcoin for long-term usage.

To illustrate, if there are currently around 464,000 daily unique bitcoin addresses used, then the estimated total value of bitcoin would be $215 billion (464,000 ^2). Bitcoin's total market value have seen some wild swings from a high of $290 billion in early January 2018 to a low of $115 billion towards the end of the first quarter of 2018.

If in the long run, the number of unique address doubles to 928,000, then the estimated total value of bitcoin may balloon to $862 billion, or around $41,000 per bitcoin. Again, this valuation is highly dependent on the *network effects* of bitcoin.

The seven network effects of bitcoin

Trace Mayer, J.D., a long-time bitcoin guru and investor in bitcoin companies such as *Armory* and *Kraken*, has explained the network effects that will lead to bitcoin's continued success in one of his early talks.

According to Mayer, the network effects of bitcoin will eventually make bitcoin a dominant world currency. The seven network effects that will continue to increase network participants and drive bitcoin prices are as follows:

1. **Speculation**. Investors are continually looking for securities or assets that can provide them above-average returns. The continued price appreciation and high volatility of bitcoin are perfect for investors with high-risk tolerance.
2. **Merchant Adoption**. Merchants will adopt systems that can improve collection, decrease costs related to payment processing, and improve their profit margins. More merchants will eventually use bitcoin to avoid credit card fees and to reduce the possibility of unwarranted chargebacks.
3. **Consumer Adoption**. Due to the improving ease of acquiring bitcoins, merchant adoption and normalization of transaction fees, more consumers will likely use bitcoins to pay for online and offline purchases. Furthermore, bitcoin is becoming the digital equivalent of gold, and it is now an acceptable means to store value. These will undoubtedly expand the bitcoin network and push the price of bitcoin higher.
4. **Security**. When bitcoin prices go up, it will incentivize more miners to participate and secure the network. The decentralized and immutability feature of the blockchain (public ledger) has led to the creation of the *three-entry bookkeeping*. This is a system of record keeping wherein debits plus credits plus the *Network Confirmations* of transactions increases trust and accountability across the network.
5. **Developer Mindshare**. Bitcoin, which was built upon the open-source concept, is a natural magnet for developers. Developers can quickly create useful apps such as payment processors, remittance services, and peer-to-peer lending without seeking permission from

77

anyone. The bitcoin network encourages innovation without permission. The lure of permission-less innovation will further increase the number of network participants. Ultimately, developers will continue to flock towards bitcoin.

6. *Financialization*. The increasing adoption of bitcoin in the field of remittance, micropayments, lending, and securities/asset exchange will lead traditional banks and other financial institutions to reconsider their business models. Unless they embrace the emerging technologies behind cryptocurrencies, financial institutions risk becoming less relevant in the years to come. Institutional adoption of bitcoin and other cryptocurrencies has already begun, and this will further introduce new participants into the network.

7. **Adoption as a World Reserve Currency**. All of the previous network effects will eventually culminate in bitcoin being a world reserve currency. Real estate transactions, stock purchases, car registrations, and other transactions of value will be settled in global blockchains that may directly or indirectly involve bitcoin. This reality will take time to achieve, but bitcoin has the potential to rival the major currencies in the future.

The bitcoin network is quickly building momentum. It is now regarded as a stable currency that thrives on the internet and frees its users from third parties. It can help merchants save money and improve consumer spending. Bitcoin is inflation-proof, and anyone can audit its code. Bitcoin developers are working tirelessly to develop the network. The above-listed network effects can only serve to strengthen it.

Valuing (Pricing) bitcoin as a currency

In an analysis published last October 2017, *dean of valuation* Aswath Damodaran, a professor of corporate finance and valuation at New York University, has argued that "bitcoin is not an asset, but a currency, and as such, you cannot value it or invest in it." He said, "You can only price it and trade it."

He pointed out that as something relatively new, it remains to be seen whether or not bitcoin can function as a store of value or an *asset*. He argued that bitcoin cannot be an *asset* because it does not promise regular future returns or cash flows. It also cannot be a *commodity* because it is not a raw material that can be used in the production of something useful. Damodaran instead suggested that bitcoin, as of this moment, is more of a *currency* but it can also be a novelty or collectible.

Value, in this context, is derived from an object's ability to generate future cash flows (returns). A good business, for example, will regularly yield future cash flows. It is *cash-generating*. Since bitcoin does not generate regular cash flows (only once when sold), Damodaran argued that it cannot be valued, it can only be *priced*. An object can acquire a *price* if people desire it (perceived demand), and it is scarce (limited). Accordingly, not everything can be valued but almost everything can be priced. Using this perspective, even a piece of worn-out jeans of a celebrity can have a *price* but will have no underlying *value*. Price is thus primarily determined by demand and supply and is affected by the market's mood and momentum.

To further explain his position, Damodaran has differentiated *investing* from *trading*. *Investing* requires decisions to be made based on an understanding of the underlying value of an asset, while *trading* is figuring out the direction of the price and making a judgment based on the potential price movement. Since bitcoin cannot be classified as an asset within Damodaran's definition, it cannot be an investment vehicle. It can, however, be *traded* since it has a price.

Therefore, to be a good bitcoin trader, one needs to use tools and techniques to analyze bitcoin's price and market sentiments which can be significantly affected by news or rumors.

A simplistic approach to *price* bitcoin in the long-term is to look into the total market capitalization of the global money supply used as a medium of exchange rather than as a store of value. At the end of 2017, *broad money*, which includes physical currencies, checking accounts, savings accounts, and money-market accounts, is estimated to total more than $80 trillion.

Assuming bitcoin will eventually capture around 5 percent of the total global money supply used as mediums of exchange, the total market capitalization of bitcoin will be at least $4 trillion. The price of each bitcoin thus may eventually reach $190,500.

Uncertainty in pricing bitcoin

The valuation (pricing) models presented above are relatively simple using optimistic assumptions. The significant price movements in bitcoin recently prove that no valuation or pricing model can accurately put a price for bitcoin in the short term. There are many unknown variables that need to be considered.

The optimistic price range for bitcoin can only be possible if the fundamental assumptions persist and that the network effects are achieved. However, there is a possibility that an alternative cryptocurrency will disrupt bitcoin's dominance, and thus reduce its network effects. This competition would undoubtedly result in lower prices for bitcoin.

Many experts agree that bitcoin will continue to grow and will become a dominant player in the world's monetary system. There is, however, a growing list of issues that bitcoin has to overcome for it to become the dominant currency.

There is a huge possibility that babies today will no longer use fiat currency when they grow up. Will bitcoin be the preferred network of the next generation? Only time can tell.

Key Points

1. The price of bitcoin remains to be very volatile.
2. The price slump that occurred early in 2018 may have been a *deflation* of the bitcoin bubble.

3. Valuing or pricing bitcoin can be very tricky because it is a relatively new instrument (asset/currency/commodity).
4. There are three main schools of thought when it comes to bitcoin *valuation* (pricing) – as an asset, a network technology, or as a currency.
5. The recovery and continued increase of bitcoin's price is highly dependent on the achievement of the bitcoin network effects.

This page is intentionally left blank.

Chapter 5

DABBLING IN BITCOIN

"When I first heard about Bitcoin, I thought it was impossible. How can you have a purely digital currency? Can't I just copy your hard drive and have your bitcoins? I didn't understand how that could be done, and then I looked into it and it was brilliant."

– Jeff Garzik, Bitcoin Core Developer and Co-Founder of Bloq, a blockchain technology company

Bitcoin Millionaire

In May 2011, 12-year-old Erik Finman decided that the best way to spend the 1,000 dollars that his loving grandmother gave him for his studies was to buy bitcoin. Bitcoin was trading at $12 apiece that time.

Erik was not a fan of the traditional education. Because of this aversion to schools, he made a bet with his parents – if he turned 18 and were a millionaire, they would not force him to go to college.

Towards the end of 2013, Erik decided to sell some of his bitcoin for $1,200 each. He then founded an online education company in 2014 for frustrated students like him to find teachers over video chat. His bitcoin earnings entirely funded the company. At age 15, he was included in Time Magazine's *The 25 Most Influential Teens of 2014*.

His online education company was subsequently sold in 2015 for $100,000 paid in bitcoins. Bitcoin's price dropped to around $200 when he sold his company. He got around 300 bitcoins in the transaction.

With several hundreds of bitcoins in his possession, then 18-year-old Erik became one of the world's youngest bitcoin millionaires when the price of one bitcoin reached $2,800 in 2017. Thus, his parents had no objection to his decision not to pursue a college degree.

At age 19, Erik's cryptocurrency portfolio continued to rise with the dramatic increase in bitcoin prices in 2017. Despite the price slump in early 2018, his portfolio remains substantial. He is currently working with NASA to launch small research satellites into space.

Erik's story is a unique tale of perseverance, dedication, and luck. His story has inspired many people to also invest in bitcoin and other cryptocurrencies. However, investing in something new will undoubtedly have some corresponding risks.

In this chapter, we will tackle the risks related to acquiring bitcoins, the ways to acquire bitcoins, how to use bitcoins, and how to store them properly.

Risks of acquiring bitcoins

At the start of 2017, mainstream media had limited coverage about bitcoin and cryptocurrencies. Towards the middle of 2017, stories of individuals making it big because of bitcoin has slowly crept into the media, and a lot of people have begun to show interest in bitcoins.

Coverage for bitcoin-related stories reached an all-time high in December 2017, the same time when the prices of bitcoin reached its peak. During this time, many people have shown interest in *investing* or speculating on bitcoin after hearing about those who became "instant millionaires." Other enterprising individuals have also created Ponzi schemes that rode on bitcoin's popularity and novelty.

In the first quarter of 2018, however, the price of bitcoin started plummeting, and those who bought bitcoin towards the end of 2017 have suffered massive losses. A lot of those 'investors' did not even understand what bitcoin is all about. Some have lost millions for participating in Ponzi schemes believing they have invested in bitcoins.

People started complaining and regulatory agencies across the world begun seriously looking into cryptocurrencies with, the aim of regulating them. Some regulatory agencies have taken active steps to regulate the emerging cryptocurrency sector of their economies supposedly to protect the investing public.

The graph shows the number of searches related to the term "bitcoin" in the United States. Interest in bitcoin peaked in December 2017 when the price of bitcoin rose to $20,000. Screenshot from Google Trends

As you may have already gleaned from the previous discussion, people acquired bitcoin primarily for speculation rather than as a medium of exchange. Unfortunately, a lot of these individuals have a very limited understanding about bitcoin. This lack of knowledge increases the risk of financial loses. Having a deeper understanding of bitcoin can help investors comprehend the inherent risks of acquiring bitcoins and gain the ability to manage those risks better.

The following bullet points summarize the inherent risks associated with bitcoin:

- **Regulatory Risk**. Governments are wary of bitcoins primarily because it can be used for money laundering, funding terrorists and other criminal acts, and tax evasion. It is natural for governments to enforce some form of regulation including restricting or outright banning of the use and sale of bitcoins. The US SEC has recently said that bitcoin is *not a security* which eliminated the possibility of bitcoin being regulated similarly as stocks.

- **Security Risk**. Although the bitcoin network has never been compromised since its inception, applications *connected* to the bitcoin network have been previously hacked causing some bitcoin holders to lose substantial amounts of their cryptocurrency. Some of the possible security risks involve fake bitcoin wallets, malware targeting bitcoin private keys stored in a computer, and hacking cryptocurrency exchanges. Since bitcoin transactions are deemed irreversible and pseudonymous, it would be hard to track the cybercriminals involved. It is almost impossible to recover lost bitcoins.

- **Insurance Risk**. Investments in cryptocurrencies are not insured. The trading of bitcoin and cryptocurrency transfers back the risk of loss from third parties (such as insurance companies) to the holder. Funds invested in cryptocurrency exchanges are also not covered by any investor protection program.

- **Fraud Risk**. People's greed for near-instantaneous returns through cryptocurrency trading will continue to be exploited by scammers. Fraudsters have used the public's lack of understanding about cryptocurrencies, and the stories of so-called "bitcoin millionaires," to defraud people by setting up Ponzi schemes. There has been an increasing number of people that are now in jail for tricking people in supposedly buying bitcoin and inviting people to be part of their "investment" schemes.

Another common type of fraud using cryptocurrencies is fake *initial coin offerings* (ICOs). An ICO is a type of fundraising activity involving the sale of cryptocurrencies called *tokens* to the public in exchange for bitcoin and other major cryptocurrencies. The people behind these ICOs promise that the tokens can be used in their platforms to purchase services or some other type of platform utility. There have been plenty of successful ICOs that resulted to the significant increase in the token prices. Those who bought the tokens in the ICO stage enjoyed massive gains.

However, there has been a proliferation of fake ICOs whereby the people behind the ICO suddenly vanish after selling a substantial amount of fake tokens. Many people participating in these fake ICO projects have ended up holding worthless tokens or no tokens at all.

- **Market Risk**. There are two significant market risks for bitcoin: first, bitcoin prices are very volatile and second, market adoption.

  Bitcoin's price continues to be very volatile. A 60 to 80 percent change in price can be considered normal for bitcoin and other cryptocurrencies. Furthermore, bitcoin prices are easily affected by news or rumors. Market sentiments can cause significant losses for speculators.

  The second type of market risk is the possibility of decreasing bitcoin adoption. As discussed in the earlier portion of this chapter, the network effects have a positive impact on bitcoin prices; however, the opposite is also true. If the network effects (e.g., global merchant and consumer adoption) are not achieved, bitcoin can become worthless. Alternative cryptocurrencies can also be considered a threat to bitcoin as these can push bitcoin prices downward.

- **Tax Risk**. The general rule on taxation is that all income earned by a citizen will be taxed. It is clear that earnings from bitcoin investments could be taxed. There is a move in many countries around the world to force their citizens to report these earnings. Some of these moves include requiring cryptocurrency exchanges that operate within the government's jurisdiction to submit the tax information, and cryptocurrency transactions of individuals who have used their services.

Since existing tax laws do not cover these types of trading activities, the earnings from cryptocurrency trading can be taxed in full. This imposition can involve a big chunk of the traders' profits (from 20 to 35 percent) plus potential penalties, interest, and surcharges.

In the investment risk continuum, bitcoin and cryptocurrency investments can be currently classified as *ultra-high risk* – a lot farther from stocks' *high-risk* label. It is but essential to put this risk in context. Cryptocurrencies have been around for only less than a decade, and people are still figuring out how they can affect the world. The future of cryptocurrencies is still very much unknown. However, the public will eventually understand how to better manage the risks involved in cryptocurrency investing just like in traditional investments.

Investment Risk Continuum

Low Risk		High Risk		Ultra-high Risk

← ————————————————————————————→

| Cash | Bonds | Stocks | Property | Derivatives | Cryptocurrency |

Acquiring bitcoin

Now that we understand the risks involved in acquiring, speculating, and trading bitcoins, let us now move on to acquiring bitcoins.

Step 1: Create a bitcoin wallet

The primary contact point for first-time bitcoin holders is the *wallet*. A bitcoin *wallet* is a software application that allows a user to store, track, send, and receive bitcoins.

Bitcoin Address

Tapping the QR code may improve scanning

1ELoBhd6mP8q
U5kLqvjn8Ztu
e16x1YQvXN

Optional Amount

0.00 BTC

Share Bitcoin Address

Copy to Clipboard

Screenshot from the author's newly-created bitcoin address using a bitcoin mobile app. The bitcoin address's QR code consists of black squares arranged in a square grid on a white background, which can be read by an imaging device such as a camera, and processed until the image can be appropriately interpreted. Below the QR code is the human-readable bitcoin address.

Bitcoin *wallets* are more like keychains because they store users' *digital keys* (*private* and *public keys*). The *private key*, also called *digital signature*, enables a user to "sign" transactions. The *public key*, from which the *bitcoin address* is derived from, is used to receive bitcoins from another bitcoin holder.

Think about the *public key* as your account number, the *bitcoin address* as the account name used to identify you as the payee in a check payable to you, and the *private key* as your signature used in a check to authorize fund transfers from your account. All of these data are stored in the bitcoin wallet software. A user will not usually see the public and private keys. Only the bitcoin address will often appear in a bitcoin wallet's interface since this is the essential information that users need to transact with other participants in the bitcoin network.

Using a wallet app, a user may create multiple *bitcoin addresses* at no cost. A bitcoin address is an identifier of 26-35 alphanumeric characters, beginning with the number 1 or 3. It enables a user to receive bitcoins from others.

This is an example of a bitcoin address:

1ELoBhd6mP8qU5kLqvjn8Ztue16x1YQvXN

This address will be used to identify the recipient of a bitcoin transaction. Bitcoin addresses are case-sensitive. Thus *quick response* (QR) *codes* are used to represent these addresses to avoid typographical errors.

Bitcoin Wallets

There are two general types of *wallet* – hot and cold wallets. *Hot wallets* store the user's information (public and private key) online, while *cold wallets* store wallet information offline. Cold wallets are generally considered more secure than hot wallets. This is because hot wallets are connected to the internet, and cybercriminals can take advantage of the devices' security vulnerabilities to steal stored digital keys.

Cold Wallets	Hot (Software) Wallets
Paper wallets Hardware wallets	Mobile wallets Desktop wallets Web wallets

Cold Wallets

1. A **paper wallet** is a piece of paper containing digital keys. It is considered the simplest of all the wallets. Storing bitcoins on paper wallets is ideal for long-term safekeeping. It is generally considered very secure since it is not connected to the internet, but it is the easiest to lose.

    Thus, storing bitcoins on paper wallets becomes unsafe unless rigorous security precautions are undertaken during their initial preparation.

Sample bitcoin paper wallet. Photo from Wikipedia

Users can quickly create a new bitcoin address and print the wallet with a printer using online services such as *WalletGenerator* and *BitcoinPaperWallet*. Users can then send some bitcoin to the newly-created bitcoin address, and store it safely or give it away. Users have to subsequently use a hot wallet to transact in the bitcoin network.

2. **Hardware wallets** are tamper-proof electronic devices designed to store digital keys in an offline setting. They are often used to store large amounts of cryptocurrencies because:

   - the specialized device has been designed to securely store the user's private keys and prevent unauthorized access to those keys;
   - they are protected from computer viruses and malware that steal from software wallets;
   - they can be used interactively to transact within the bitcoin network, unlike paper wallets which must be imported to a software wallet at some point; and
   - the software is often open-source, allowing a user to validate the entire operation of the device.

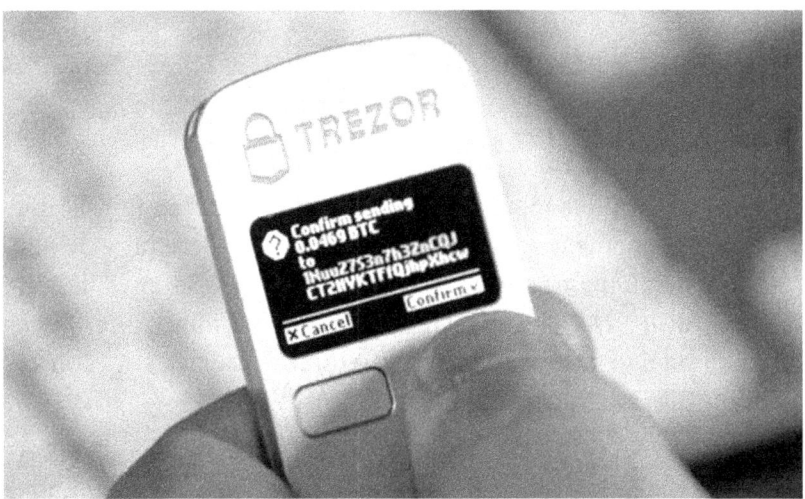

Detailed photo of TREZOR hardware wallet showing transaction details on its display. Photo from Wikipedia

Some of the most famous hardware wallets are:

- *KeepKey*
- *Ledger Nano S*
- *Trezor*
- *Digital Bitbox*

A hardware wallet is considered the safest, but is also the most expensive way of storing bitcoins. When purchasing hardware wallets, it is essential to buy from authorized sellers. Hardware wallets obtained from dubious sources may be compromised.

Hot Wallets

1. **Mobile wallets** are mobile applications for smartphones that store wallet data within the mobile device. They are easy-to-use and reliable, while also being secure and fast. A mobile app is an excellent choice for non-technical people because it can be conveniently used to pay for something in bitcoin in a shop, buy, sell, or send while on the move. Mobile wallets are free to download, and most wallets have both Android and iOS versions.

   Some of the famous mobile wallets are *Bitcoin Wallet, Bither, breadwallet, Electrum, GreenBits, Mycelium, Airbitz, ArcBit, Coin.Space, Green Address*, and *Simple Bitcoin Wallet*.

2. **Desktop wallets** require users to download and install the software directly on the users' computer. These wallets provide the user more flexibility to control the digital keys. Desktop wallets are free to download, and are relatively easy to configure. However, the additional control provided by desktop wallets also comes with some disadvantages.

   The user has to perform backups and other maintenance tasks. Aside from the usual memory requirements, some desktop wallets occupy a big chunk of a user's hard drive since they also act as nodes for the bitcoin network. As of April 2018, a user needs to allocate at least 164 gigabytes of hard disk space to fully run a bitcoin desktop wallet. Furthermore, if the user's computer gets stolen, corrupted, or hacked, the digital keys may be compromised resulting in your bitcoins being lost or stolen.

Some of the famous desktop wallets are *Bitcoin Core* (the first desktop wallet), *ArcBit, Bitcoin Knots, Electrum, Green Address, mSIGNA, Armory*, and *Bither.* As you may have noticed, some of these desktop wallets also have corresponding mobile wallets.

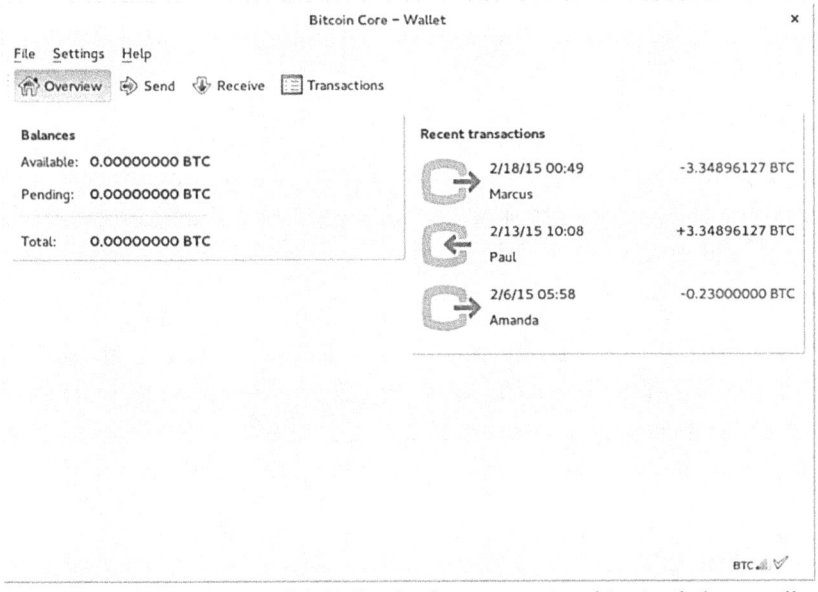

Screenshot of Bitcoin core (v0.10.0), the longest-running bitcoin desktop wallet. Photo from Wikipedia

3. A **web wallet**, also known as *online* or *cloud-based wallet*, offers users convenience because they can easily access their bitcoin funds from any device with the use of passwords and two-factor authentication (2FA). Web wallets are easy to set-up, and some have desktop and mobile versions which make it easy to spend and receive bitcoin.

Some bitcoin web wallets are linked to cryptocurrency exchanges (such as Coinbase) that make it easier to trade other cryptocurrencies. Other wallets also provide additional security features including the ability for users to store their digital keys in offline storages.

Just like mobile wallets, the conveniences that come with web wallets also create corresponding risks. Web wallets store users' digital keys in their servers. This means that users have to trust the web wallet providers' security measures and their overall reputation.

Coinbase, Blockchain.info, BitGo, Coinapult, Coin.Space, and *Green Address* are famous for providing web wallets.

Which wallet should a prospective user choose?

As a new bitcoin user, it would be best to initially involve only a small amount of fiat currency, and gradually increase the transaction size as you build confidence. This to minimize the risk of loss in the rare instance that you make a mistake.

Since the risk is relatively small when dealing with a small amount of funds, you can use a mobile or web wallet which is considered the fastest and easiest way to acquire bitcoins. For mobile wallets, search for a bitcoin wallet that has significant downloads and relatively high-rating.

If you prefer a web wallet, you can open an account with any of the web wallet service providers earlier mentioned in this section. Most of these wallet service providers would require an email address while others may require additional information as part of their know-your-customer (KYC) procedures. Some wallets may even need an ID selfie where the user has to take a selfie while holding their valid ID card. Once you complete the KYC procedure, you would become a *verified user*. *Verified users* have fewer transaction restrictions which means they can transact more significant amounts of fiat currency and bitcoin.

Opening an account would only take a few minutes. A wallet that also has a significant presence or office where you are located should be a crucial factor in deciding which wallet you would use. This is because there may be more funding options to choose from if the wallet you have chosen has a local bank or cash-in partner.

Best practices in keeping your wallet secure

Use only trustworthy wallet service providers. Dubious wallet service providers, and even some large cryptocurrency exchanges, have been previously compromised, and their users' digital keys have been stolen. Thus, it is vital that you choose providers that have proven track-records.

Just like having multiple bank accounts, putting your funds in multiple wallets is also recommended. Keep your cryptocurrencies in various places. For example, put a small amount on your mobile and web wallet for transaction purposes, and keep the bulk of your cryptocurrencies in multiple hardware wallets.

Enable two-factor authentication (2FA). When using hot wallets, always enable 2FA. It is an extra layer of security known as *multi-factor authentication* which requires not only a password and username but also something that only the user has access to like a single-use code sent to the user's registered email address or mobile number. By requiring a piece of information (i.e., the single-use code) that only the user knows, hackers will have a hard time attempting to gain access, and steal the user's digital keys.

Most wallets will require the user to enable 2FA to transact with a higher amount.

Backup your wallets. Having a backup of your wallets can protect you from sudden hardware failures and other mistakes. Some mobile wallets let users backup their wallet by giving them access to the digital keys stored in the device. The users can then write down the digital keys, which can be used in another mobile device, to

---

recover the users' credentials.

Other mobile wallets use *mnemonic phrase* to backup users' digital keys. Also called *mnemonic seed*, the *mnemonic phrase* is a list of several words which store all the information needed to recover a wallet. Mnemonic phrases are considered a standard way of backing up wallets. A user can use this mnemonic phrase to restore his/her digital keys on another device using the same wallet software in case the user's computer breaks or its hard drive becomes corrupted. However, anybody can also use the same phrase to steal the bitcoins stored using the keys linked to the phrase. It is a good idea then to keep the paper, where the mnemonic phrase is written, in a secure location.

Keep your software wallet updated. It is crucial that you keep your wallet software always updated. Updates often include security and bug fixes that will ensure your digital keys remain safe. It can also include new useful features. Keeping your computer or mobile phone's operating system and other software applications updated can further enhance the security of the environment in which your wallet software operates in.

Require multi-signature (multisig). If you are dealing with shared funds or organizational funds, it is a good idea to enable the multisig feature. This feature, available to some bitcoin wallets, requires multiple independent approvals to spend the bitcoin stored in a wallet.

Important Note: It is a wise idea to have a plan to let your family members or peers gain access to your digital keys when you pass away. Unlike money in banks, real estate, and other physical assets, your cryptocurrencies can be lost forever if no one knows your password or where you placed your wallet software backups. So it is essential to think about these matters when converting substantial amounts of your wealth into bitcoins or other cryptocurrencies.

Step 2: Funding your wallet

Once you have created a bitcoin wallet, the next step is to fund your wallet with bitcoins.

There are four basic ways to acquire bitcoins:

1. Mine bitcoin
2. Earn from bitcoin faucets
3. Get paid in bitcoin
4. Buy bitcoin

Mine bitcoin

In the previous chapter, we talked about how difficult it is to mine bitcoin in your home today. However, mining bitcoin was the easiest way to acquire bitcoin in the early years of the bitcoin network. Simply download a bitcoin mining software, and let it run. The mined bitcoins will then be credited to your bitcoin wallet.

People who are interested in bitcoin mining should possess technical skills and, more importantly, the funds to successfully operate a bitcoin mining facility. The difficulty of the mathematical challenges in bitcoin mining now requires specialized machines (ASICs). Aside from the ASIC's limited utility, these machines can be costly to purchase and maintain. Starting mining operations without the proper knowledge will undoubtedly result in financial losses.

An alternative to independently mining bitcoins is joining mining pools or investing in cloud mining services. Joining a mining pool also requires some technical know-how and the right equipment to become profitable. Cloud mining platforms require significant cash investments and many of these platforms are masquerading scams.

Hence, mining bitcoin is not recommended for beginners. If you wish to tread this path, it is vital that you do your research properly.

Refer to the previous chapter for more details on bitcoin mining.

Bitcoin faucets

Before the significant price escalation experienced in 2017, people got a lot of satoshis (1 satoshi = 0.00000001 bitcoin) for performing tasks, viewing ads, solving puzzles, playing online games, downloading apps, or giving away their email addresses. Websites or apps that enable users to earn a few satoshis by simply doing these activities are called *bitcoin faucets*.

A factor in driving the price of a cryptocurrency is the number of people using the cryptocurrency's network. Running bitcoin faucets has been a great way to distribute bitcoins which increases the number of network participants. These faucets were also used as a creative means of converting bitcoins earned by miners or early cryptocurrency enthusiasts into fiat currency or useable data (e.g., potential client email addresses). Today, bitcoin faucets are commonly used to advertise products and services online.

Because bitcoin's price has significantly increased, some bitcoin faucets stopped using bitcoin and shifted to other cryptocurrencies. However, there is still a significant number of bitcoin faucets that distribute a few satoshis for performing their required tasks.

As a beginner, you can try doing tasks in a bitcoin faucet. However, do not expect to earn a significant amount of bitcoins. Most of these bitcoin faucets require their users to sign-up to their website, provide a bitcoin address, and accumulate a certain amount of bitcoin before they allow you to withdraw the satoshis you earned. Today, you can earn the equivalent of a few cents of bitcoin for several hours or a few days' worth of tasks, but it is a good way to begin dabbling in bitcoin.

Get paid in bitcoin

Another way to acquire bitcoin is by selling goods or providing services for bitcoins. An increasing number of online and offline merchants have started accepting bitcoins as a payment option.

Merchants can directly receive bitcoin payment using their bitcoin addresses. There are also merchants that make use of third-party bitcoin payment processors like *Bitpay* to generate bitcoin addresses, accept and confirm payments, and issue invoices intuitively and seamlessly. *Bitpay* can easily be integrated into a website just like *Paypal*.

There are also some websites that pay bitcoin to freelancers. Some of the notable bitcoin-first freelancing sites are *XBTFreelancer*, *Reddit's Jobs4Bitcoins* page, and *Coinality*. Bitcoin is becoming a preferred payment option for the salaries of freelancers and other remote workers because of bitcoin's convenience and speed. Furthermore, an increasing number of wallets and exchanges make bitcoin readily convertible to fiat.

Buying bitcoins

For a beginner, buying bitcoins will be the simplest way to acquire bitcoin. You can buy bitcoin through:

Online options

1. A wallet app/software
2. A cryptocurrency exchange

Offline options

3. A bitcoin ATM
4. A purchase meetup (person-to-person buying)

Buying through a wallet or cryptocurrency exchange

The easiest way to acquire bitcoin is to purchase it using a mobile or web wallet that allows buying bitcoin using their platform. You can also open an account with a *cryptocurrency exchange* that supports fiat funding. *Cryptocurrency exchanges* will automatically create users' bitcoin wallet and the addresses.

Some bitcoin wallets and cryptocurrency exchanges allow their users to enroll and fund their account using a credit card. Funding your wallet or account using a credit card is often considered costly because of the credit card fees that range from 1 to 5 percent. Other bitcoin wallets and exchanges also allow various cash-in options including international money transfers (remittance), bank deposits, and through their network of collection agencies.

To avoid multiple conversion fees, it is best to open an account or create a wallet that supports your preferred currency.

Funding a wallet or an account in a cryptocurrency exchange using a credit card only takes a few seconds. However, funding your wallet using other methods may take some time usually from 1 to 3 days. Once the wallet has confirmed the funding, the amount will appear in your dashboard in fiat values. The amount can then be used to purchase bitcoins using the "buy" or "convert" feature of the wallet.

After buying or converting your fiat deposit in the wallet, the bitcoins will subsequently be transferred to the bitcoin address created by your wallet or exchange. If you did everything correctly, you should now see the amount of bitcoin in your wallet.

Cryptocurrency Exchanges

A *cryptocurrency exchange* is similar to a money changer where currencies are sold for another currency. *Cryptocurrency exchanges* are websites that are run by companies that allow their users to buy and sell cryptocurrencies. The main benefit of exchanges is that it provides liquidity to the cryptocurrency ecosystem. Cryptocurrency traders and investors can easily buy and sell their cryptocurrencies, then subsequently convert them to fiat currency.

Most exchanges provide technical trading tools to their users for them to analyze prices and charts. These cryptocurrency platforms earn through commissions and other exchange fees.

Some of the largest cryptocurrency exchanges are *Binance, Huobi, Upbit, OKEx, Bithumb, Poloniex, Bittrex* and *Kraken*.

The topic on cryptocurrency exchange will be discussed at length in my next book on cryptocurrency investing. Sign up to my mailing list to get updates and discounts: **https://cryptocurrency101.ph/subscribe**

Buying via bitcoin ATMs

A two-way Bitcoin ATM at Decentral in Toronto that allows users to buy or sell bitcoins with cash. Photo from Wikipedia

Recently, a lot of bitcoin automated teller machines (ATM) have been set up in various places. These bitcoin ATMs dispense bitcoins after receiving fiat currency. A bitcoin ATM is a device connected to the internet that allows an individual to exchange bitcoins and fiat currency. Most bitcoin ATMs offer one-way functionality, enabling only the purchase of bitcoin for cash. Others provide more advanced features including dispensing cash for bitcoins sold using the machine. These machines connect users directly to a cryptocurrency exchange instead of a bank account. *Coin ATM Radar* estimates that there are almost 3,000 bitcoin ATMs across the world.

The use of the term "ATM" is a misnomer since there are no "tellers" in the cryptocurrency ecosystem. The term has been coined because they look similar to bank ATMs. It has also been used to simplify the concept behind the machine.

Users show their bitcoin address in QR code format using their mobile wallets. Then, the machine scans the QR code and checks the format of the bitcoin address. The user will need to insert cash into the bitcoin ATM or kiosk, wait for confirmation, and receive a receipt for the transaction.

Bitcoin purchase meetups

Beginners may also want to personally purchase bitcoins from a local seller. This option may also be the case if there are no bitcoin ATMs or other funding options for your mobile or web wallet.

There are reliable websites that enable this type of person-to-person transactions. One of the oldest and trusted sites is *LocalBitcoins.com*.

LocalBitcoins.com, which has been established in 2012, is a person-to-person bitcoin trading site. The site enables people from different countries to exchange their local fiat currency to bitcoins. Users create an account and post advertisements stating the price of bitcoin they are willing to buy or sell as well as their preferred payment methods. Other users then respond to these advertising posts and agree to meet in person to exchange cash or trade directly through online banking.

To prevent fraud, the seller is required to place the bitcoins to be sold in *LocalBitcoins.com*'s web wallet. Once the transaction has been confirmed, the bitcoins are then transferred to the purchaser's wallet. The website also has a reputation and feedback mechanism and conflict-resolution service for users.

Localbitcoins.com automatically recognizes the user's IP address and will display relevant results based on the user's location.

What funding method should you choose?

The funding method you will use shall heavily depend on your current circumstances, amount of bitcoin you are purchasing, and the crypto-currency environment in your area or region. Some of these methods may not be suitable for you. Other methods may be suitable for you but may not be available. You have to do your research, and test out a few of the options to find out which one fits your requirements.

Using bitcoin

Now that you are a proud owner of several satoshis, what will you do with these bitcoins? With the growing acceptance of bitcoin, holders can now do more with their bitcoins.

Here are some ways you can use your bitcoins:

1. **Buy goods and services from various online and offline merchants**. Some of the most famous companies that accept bitcoin are online travel agency *Expedia*, website content management system *Wordpress*, software powerhouse *Microsoft*, computer maker *Dell*, fast-food chain *KFC Canada*, online retailer *Overstock*, online community *Reddit*, content creator *Playboy*, sandwich maker *Subway*, online newspaper *Bloomberg.com*, and e-commerce platform *Shopify*, among others. Aside from the several thousands of online stores, there are over a hundred thousand physical stores today that accept bitcoin.

2. **Hold bitcoin as a long-term investment.** If you believe that the price of bitcoin will continue to rise over the long-term, you can purchase bitcoins today and wait for the price to rise. As an investment, it is crucial that you properly understand the risks related to bitcoin ownership. We learned about the risks earlier in this chapter. You should also be able to manage these risks better.

   Also, keep in mind the best practices in storing bitcoins as discussed earlier in this chapter.

3. **Trade cryptocurrencies.** Persons with higher risk tolerance can consider trading bitcoin and other cryptocurrencies for short-term gains. You can do this in cryptocurrency exchanges. The largest cryptocurrency exchanges require their users to deposit bitcoin first before they can trade within their platform. Bitcoin is the *default* currency used in exchanges.

Trading cryptocurrencies can lead to significant losses. It is sage advice that you only trade cryptocurrencies if you are prepared to lose all of your funds. The following table summarizes the difference between investing and trading:

Cryptocurrency Investing vs. Trading

Factor	Investing	Trading
Purpose	Develop and grow an investment portfolio over the longer term	Generate short-term cash flow
Time Frame	Medium to long-term (typically between 1 month and many years)	Short to medium term (usually between 1 hour and a few months)
Leverage (use of credit)	Never or in a limited capacity	Yes, very frequently
Timing	Less important	Critically important
Type of play	Research-driven / Investment analysis	e.g., Momentum play (technical analysis)
What is analyzed	Cryptocurrency utility and technology (fundamentals)	Charts and patterns
Activity	Usually Passive	Active
Famous Saying	Rule No. 1 – don't lose money Rule No. 2 – don't forget Rule no. 1	The trend is your friend until it ends

If you wish to learn more about cryptocurrency investing and trading, you can check out my next book to be released later in 2018. Subscribe to my mailing list at cryptocurrency101.ph/subscribe to get updates about my upcoming book.

4. **Donate to charity.** Using bitcoin and other cryptocurrencies to donate funds to charitable causes is becoming more common. There are many nonprofit organizations embracing cryptocurrencies as a cost-efficient manner to receive donations. Some of the charities that accept bitcoin are *Wikipedia / Wikimedia*, *Electronic Frontier Foundation* (*EFF*), the *Water Project*, and the *Internet Archive*.

5. **Convert into gift cards.** Bitcoin holders can easily purchase online gift cards from various merchants and send it to the intended recipients via email. Online marketplace *Gyft* offers bitcoin holders the ability to buy gift cards from many big companies including *Amazon*, *App Store*, *eBay*, and *Best Buy*.

6. **Give some away.** The probability of bitcoin becoming a globally-accepted currency is significantly dependent on the number of network participants. You can do your part by teaching other people how to use bitcoin, and giving them some bitcoins. By doing this, you can also increase your confidence in doing transactions in the bitcoin network. Get your friend to install a bitcoin wallet and transfer a small amount to the newly-created wallet to get them started!

Key Points

1. There are several inherent risks to be considered when acquiring bitcoins. These are regulatory risk, security risk, fraud risk, market risk and tax risk.
2. Bitcoin users need to understand the risks to protect themselves from financial losses better.

3. The first task of a new bitcoin user is to create a wallet. There are two general kinds of bitcoin wallet – cold and hot wallet.
4. It is the responsibility of the bitcoin user to protect their wallets.
5. There are several ways to acquire bitcoins. These include mining, earning from bitcoin faucets, receiving bitcoin payments and buying bitcoins.
6. Buying bitcoin is probably the easiest way to acquire bitcoin for beginners.
7. There are many ways to use bitcoin including buying merchandise, holding it as an investment, trading other cryptocurrencies, donating to charity, converting it into gift cards, and educating others by giving some away.

Chapter 6

A VARIETY OF CRYPTOCURRENCIES

"Blockchain is the tech. Bitcoin is merely the first mainstream manifestation of its potential."

– Marc Kenigsberg, Blockchain and Cryptocurrency Advocate

In 2015, Vitalik Buterin, a young Canadian programmer, realized that the technology behind bitcoin has more potential. He then started building a new blockchain that can be used as a platform and not merely a currency.

From then on, people started building various projects using blockchain as the core technology. These projects have various potential real-world uses including platforms for building decentralized applications, storage, fundraising, identity verification, notarial services, and tokenization or digitization of physical assets.

Programmers and entrepreneurs realized that they could build programs that solve real-world challenges without the need for significant capital or permission from central authorities. An entirely new and global application or network can be created within a few months if you know how to code. The ease of development has ushered in a new wave of blockchain projects and cryptocurrencies related to those projects.

There are currently over 1,600 cryptocurrencies that have been created. Each cryptocurrency is trying to solve different problems. In this chapter, we will focus on some of the major cryptocurrencies that can have a significant impact on society.

Classification of Cryptocurrencies

We can classify cryptocurrencies into three (3) broad categories based on their uses:

a. Value transfer (currency)
b. Platform
c. Specialized uses

Under each classification, many cryptocurrencies have been developed either on top of an existing blockchain or on an entirely new one. We will discuss some of the notable cryptocurrencies under each category.

Value Transfer (Currency Use)

We have extensively discussed the definition of currency in the previous chapters of this book. Simply put, a currency is a medium of exchange – a tool to transfer value. A cryptocurrency is considered a currency if it is primarily used for peer-to-peer payments or value exchanges.

Bitcoin, often shortened as *BTC*, is one example. Many experts, however, consider bitcoin not only as a medium of exchange but primarily as a store of value like gold.

Here are some other cryptocurrencies that function as currency:

1. **Litecoin (LTC) – The faster bitcoin**
    Litecoin is considered one of the major cryptocurrencies with over $7 billion market capitalization. It was launched in 2011 by Charlie Lee, a former Google engineer. Also recognized as one of the oldest cryptocurrencies, litecoin is often said to be the equivalent of 'silver' to bitcoin's 'gold.'

    Litecoin is very similar to bitcoin since its source code has been derived from bitcoin's. The source code is a listing of commands that makes up a program or application. Most cryptocurrencies' source codes are open-source, meaning anyone can freely copy, modify, and create an entirely new blockchain for a cryptocurrency using the source code without getting the consent of the author.

Similar to bitcoin, litecoin was created as a global payment system that is not controlled by any central authority. The big difference lies in the fact that litecoin is four times (4x) faster than bitcoins. Being one of the more established cryptocurrencies, litecoin also has a significant number of merchants and users just like bitcoin.

2. Zcash (ZEC) – A more private bitcoin alternative

Zcash is considered a more secure and private cryptocurrency compared to bitcoin and litecoin. It was launched in 2016 and is currently maintained by a group of computer scientists and engineers headed by Zooko Wilcox.

The main differentiating feature of zcash as a currency is that it offers an extra layer of privacy. All zcash transactions are publicly recorded and published on its ledger just like bitcoin, but the details relating to the sender, the recipient, and the amount remain private.

Users of zcash can opt to be transparent or use the *shield* option when making transactions within the network. Shielded transactions are encrypted using zcash's advanced cryptographic technique called *zero-knowledge proof of construction*. Zcash claims that this unique technology allows the network to maintain a secure ledger of balances without disclosing the parties or amounts involved.

3. Dash – A powerful alternative to bitcoin

Originally known as Darkcoin, Dash (short for "digital cash") is a more secretive version of bitcoin. Launched five years after bitcoin in 2014, dash was created and developed by Evan Duffield and is maintained by a mix of known and anonymous developers.

Similar to zcash, dash was the first cryptocurrency to offer anonymity, and an option to send transactions privately. Dash transactions are also much faster. A typical dash transaction is validated in a few minutes which is already a lot faster than bitcoin. Dash also offers an *InstantSend* feature that validates transactions in a few seconds.

Dash started using the ticker code DASH in March 2015. It is known as one of the most successful cryptocurrency re-brandings that aim to make dash appeal to more users and remove the misconception that they are part of the dark web which is predominantly accessed and used by criminals.

4. Monero (XMR) – A completely anonymous cryptocurrency

At almost the same time as dash, monero was launched in 2014 by an anonymous developer with the pseudonym *thankful_for_today*. A group of mostly pseudonymous programmers now maintains it. Just like the other cryptocurrencies, monero also offers itself as a more secure and private alternative to bitcoin.

Monero is known as the most private of all major cryptocurrencies because of its non-traceability feature which is inherent in the network. It uses a mix of technology founded on a unique technique called *ring signatures* that makes it impossible to link real-world identities to transactions in monero's ledger. Unlike dash and zcash, monero's development is entirely donation-based and community-driven.

Aside from being completely private, monero is considered a faster alternative to bitcoin with a similar transaction validation time as litecoin.

Platform Use

There is a new breed of applications being developed today that are not owned by any single entity, cannot be shut down, and have no downtime. These applications are called *decentralized applications* or *DApps*.

There is an increasing number of specialized cryptocurrency networks that act as platform-enabling developers to create and run DApps.

What Are DApps?

DApps are special types of software programs that run on a blockchain and use smart contracts to achieve decentralization.

Smart contracts or *digital vending machines* are programs that execute the agreement between two parties on the blockchain precisely as programmed. Smart contracts can be designed to facilitate the exchange of value which can result in the creation of a new self-executing, fully-independent application environment. Hence, no single entity can exercise control over DApps.

DApps are beneficial because it gives users control over their data without having it stored, managed, and analyzed by a central authority. Facebook has been heavily criticized for its complicit role in the *Cambridge Analytica scandal* which led to the improper use of Facebook users' private information. This recent privacy scandal illustrates the problem with most applications today – users' private data can easily be used by central authorities for their benefit even without the users' consent.

Being decentralized, DApps users will have complete control over their data because no central entity is in charge of any users' data.

To be called a DApp, the application must meet the following requirements:

- The application's source code must be available to interested developers to allow greater scrutiny (*open-sourced*);
- Users' data should be cryptographically stored in a public and decentralized blockchain (*decentralized*);
- The application has its own tokens/digital assets (native currency) that are used to reward network participants (*incentivized*); and
- The incentive tokens are created using a cryptographic consensus algorithm to demonstrate proof of value, e.g., proof-of-work or proof-of-stake (*protocol*).

The following are some of the well-known and emerging DApps platforms:

1. Ethereum (ETH) – The Dominant DApp Platform

Ethereum is a decentralized software platform that enables smart contracts and DApps to be built and run on its network without any downtime, fraud, control or interference from a third party. It was launched in 2015 by Vitalik Buterin, who was 21 years old at that time.

Ethereum's technology is the first and most well-developed network for facilitating the development of DApps. Developers can build DApps on just about anything using *Solidity* which is Ethereum's own programming language. The DApps that have been produced so far speak volumes to where this part of the ecosystem can take us.

Developers use Ethereum's native token called *ether* to develop and run applications using Ethereum's blockchain. The network currently runs a proof-of-work algorithm to issue ethers, but there are plans to migrate to a hybrid algorithm making use of both proof-of-work and proof-of-stake.

Ethereum currently holds the number 2 spot in terms of market capitalization.

2. Ethereum classic (ETC) – The original ethereum

Ethereum Classic is also a decentralized platform that runs smart contracts. It is a derivative of the original ethereum platform and is a continuation of the original ethereum blockchain.

In June 2016, hackers were able to steal $50 million from a crowdfunding project called the *decentralized autonomous organization* (The DAO), which was built on the original ethereum blockchain. The hackers exploited a vulnerability in the DAO code that enabled them to siphon off one-third of The DAO's funds. To return the lost funds, a software upgrade, called a *hard fork*, was implemented causing a split in the ethereum's community.

Those who rejected the hard fork due to philosophical reasons decided to keep using the original version of ethereum. They argue that ethereum should be *immutable* which means the blockchain should remain unchanged regardless of the impact. Thus, ethereum classic runs the original, *classic* version preserving untampered history before the fork, and is free from external interference.

3. NEO – China's ethereum

Similar to ethereum, NEO is a blockchain platform used to build scalable network decentralized applications. NEO supports a wide variety of commonly used programming languages such as *Java*, *Javascript*, *C++*, *C#*, and soon *Python* and *Go*, making it an easily-accessible option to startups with big ideas.

Da Hongfei of the development company *Onchain* provided the initial development resources for *AntShares*, NEO's predecessor, in 2014. AntShares was eventually rebranded to NEO in June 2017.

NEO is often called *China's ethereum* because it is very similar to ethereum, mainly as a host of DApps and smart contracts. China's government fully supports it. The Chinese government's support has made NEO immensely popular among Chinese DApps developers.

4. QTUM – The mobile-focused smart contracts platform

Qtum (pronounced as *quantum*) was born as a result of a successful ICO in March 2017. It is an open-sourced value transfer platform which focuses on mobile DApps. Qtum aims to be the world's premier smart contract platform for mobile software.

The creators of qtum envisioned it to be a bridge between bitcoin and ethereum's functionalities – bitcoin's value transfer capabilities and ethereum's smart contracts platform. This blend makes qtum highly reliable and able to run any code or DApp on its blockchain without any single point of failure. Qtum is also the world's first proof-of-stake (POS) smart contracts platform.

It has been developed by the Qtum Foundation, based in Singapore, and is being headed by a team of developers led by Patrick Dai, Neil Mahi, and Jordan Earls.

5. **Cardano (ADA) – The research-driven smart contracts platform**

Cardano is a decentralized public blockchain and cryptocurrency project, and is also fully open-source. It is currently developing a smart contract platform which seeks to deliver more advanced features than any protocol previously developed. Cardano claims to be the first blockchain platform to evolve out of scientific philosophy and a research-first driven approach. The development team consists of three organizations with an extensive global collective of expert engineers and researchers.

The programming language used in Cardano is *Haskell*, a language widely used for business applications and data analysis. Cardano is expected to be likely used for financial and organizational applications.

Coins vs. Tokens

People often use the terms *coin* and *token* interchangeably when referring to cryptocurrencies. However, there are some technical differences. In fact, cryptocurrency market tracker *Coinmarketcap.com* classifies cryptocurrencies either as a coin or token.

Coins refer to cryptocurrencies that have their own blockchain. Some of these coins include bitcoin, ethereum, litecoin, ripple, and monero. They can function as currency, platform or for a specific utility.

Tokens, on the other hand, are cryptocurrencies that were issued on an existing blockchain. These tokens are used as rewards and as payment for transaction fees in DApps that operate within an existing blockchain.

An excellent example of a token is *Golem Network Tokens* (GNT). The tokens are hosted on ethereum's network. GNTs are required to use the Golem DApp, a decentralized platform where users can lease computing power from other users.

Thus, coins can exist independently unlike tokens that cannot exist without the infrastructure of a coin.

It is to be noted, however, that the difference between coins and tokens are becoming more complex with some cryptocurrencies having both the features of a coin and a token.

Specialized Uses

Some cryptocurrencies have been created for particular uses. They have their own blockchain, may operate within an existing cryptocurrency's platform, or use an entirely different system.

The following are some of those notable examples.

1. Siacoin (SC) – A decentralized cloud storage platform

Siacoin (shortened to *sia*) is a decentralized storage platform secured by blockchain technology. The sia platform provides a decentralized cloud storage similar to DropBox, Amazon, Apple, and Microsoft.

The network acts as a marketplace for storage that runs without an intermediary. Sia secures storage transactions with smart contracts, creating a more reliable and affordable offering compared to traditional cloud providers. Anyone can host or access encrypted storage using Sia's platform, and all contracts, storage proofs, and transactions are verifiable using the blockchain's public ledger. Furthermore, no centralized entity can censor or deny access to data.

Established by Boston-based *Nebulous Inc.* in 2014, siacoin's developers want siacoin's network to become the backbone storage layer of the internet. David Vorick and Luke Champine lead the team behind sia.

2. Civic (CVC) – An identity management platform on the blockchain

Civic is a blockchain-based identity management service that allows users to protect and authorize the use of their identity in real-time. Through its unique system, civic can reduce the need for recurring background and personal information verification checks.

The platform's users will be able to use their digital devices (smartphones and tablets) for streamlined identity verification checks. These devices will contain individuals' personal information, such as their names or passport numbers, so that they can quickly identify themselves at various places that require identification such as airport check-in counters, security checkpoints, and hotels. Furthermore, civic uses smart contracts that run on the blockchain for information requestors and identity validators to securely validate the identity of the user.

Civic's token sale was completed in 2017. It is backed by Vinny Lingham, a South African entrepreneur, who founded the online retail company *Gyft*.

3. Golem (GNT) – A globally-shared supercomputer

Golem aims to connect users with idle computing power with those who need it through its infrastructure powered by the ethereum network. It seeks to enable machines around the world to transact computing power with each other. It is a peer-to-peer marketplace for computing resources. Unused or excess computing resources can be rented out to users wishing to perform memory-intensive tasks including data analysis, machine learning, and CGI rendering. Users pay the renters using GNTs. According to their website, any user ranging from a single PC owner to a large data center, can share resources through Golem and get paid in GNT by requestors.

Golem is based in Poland, and its team is headed by Julian Zawistowski who also advises *OmiseGo* (OMG), another cryptocurrency project. It is considered as one of the most successful ICOs on the ethereum blockchain having raised over $8 million in a matter of minutes in 2016.

4. Ripple (XRP) – Real-time global payments network

Ripple, the largest company-backed cryptocurrency, aims to be used by banks as a real-time global settlement network. It offers instant, precise, and low-cost international payments by acting as a bridge currency to other currencies.

Co-founded in 2012 by Chris Larsen and Jed McCaleb, XRP enables banks to settle cross-border payments in real time, with end-to-end transparency, and at lower costs. Ripple's primary focus is to be used by large financial institutions like banks and payment providers because they have built their network for enterprises.

Unlike bitcoin and other cryptocurrencies, the ripple network does not need mining. Instead, they implement a so-called consensus-based ledger to verify transactions. Sans mining, the ripple network does not require substantial use of computing power.

XRP saw tremendous growth in price in 2017, and has become one of the largest cryptocurrencies in terms of market capitalization. Ripple is often criticized for being centralized which goes against the ideals for which cryptocurrency was created.

Conclusion

With over 1,600 cryptocurrencies, the list presented above is not exhaustive. However, you may glean from the previous discussions that the creation of bitcoin has spun other cryptocurrencies, each aiming to solve a particular problem.

A lot of the cryptocurrencies in the market will eventually fail. Nevertheless, the cryptocurrencies identified above, and other cryptocurrency projects that are currently being developed that have significant user bases and existing services, will continue to grow and may create a new industry or replace an existing one.

Looking at the current trend, it is clear that cryptocurrencies are here to stay and will undoubtedly continue to change the world.

Key Points

1. Cryptocurrencies can have different uses.
2. There are three broad categories of cryptocurrencies based on their use – value transfer (currency), platform and specialized uses.
3. Apps that are built on a blockchain and are not controlled by any single entity are called decentralized applications (DApps).
4. Some cryptocurrencies are classified as tokens. Tokens exist on an existing cryptocurrency infrastructure.

Message from the Author

Thanks for reading this humble work. I hope it has inspired you to explore the world of cryptocurrency further!

Sign Up!

I am currently working on a few more books and if you want to be informed about the next book, please sign up to our mailing list. You can sign up using this link:

www.cryptocurrency101.ph/subscribe

You can also get freebies, discounts and other exciting prizes if you sign up. Rest assured that we will not sell or share your contact information and will only use these to send updates and other

Invite me for a Talk

You can send me an invitation to speak at your event via email at kevin@cryptocurrency101.ph.

Support Us

We are intensifying our cryptocurrency education campaign to properly educate the public about cryptocurrency. If you want to support us in this endeavor, please let us know by sending us an email at:

info@cryptocurrency101.ph

General Inquiries

If you have any inquiries about this book, you can reach us via:

- Email: info@cryptocurrency101.ph
- Office: 1Punch Inc., Basement 2 Jose Miguel Bldg. 1, #1 Yandoc St. cor. Naguilian Road, Baguio City, Philippines 2600
- Telephone: +63 074 665 6024

About the Author

KEVIN PHILIP D. GAYAO is the Chief Executive Officer (CEO) of 1Punch Inc., a sales, training, and marketing firm based in the Philippines. He is a Certified Bitcoin Professional (CBP), a Certified Public Accountant (CPA), a Registered Cost Accountant (RCA), a Certified Accounting Technician (CAT), and a holder of a Master's Degree in Business Administration (MBA).

Kevin graduated Cum Laude with a degree in Accountancy from Saint Louis University, Philippines. He received his MBA degree from the Swiss Management Center University based in Zug, Switzerland.

Aside from managing their company, he enjoys reading mostly non-fiction books in his spare time. He is a regular speaker on cryptocurrency, investing, personal finance, and accounting.

You can connect with him through Linkedin via this link: https://www.linkedin.com/in/kpdgayao

Index

BONUS ARTICLE

Blockchain and Smart Contracts
Ushering in a New Age of Smart Contracts

Imagine a world where you can do business without trusting anyone – a world where you do not fear that the other party will not deliver on their commitment; a world that has systems that will execute contracts as they have been agreed upon, with no possibility of default, where you do not have to rely on tedious court proceedings or other third parties to decide upon the fate of your transactions.

This is the promise of smart contracts on the blockchain. And it is slowly becoming a reality.

This "trustless" reality began to unfold on the 3rd of January 2009, when Satoshi Nakamoto successfully exchanged value without using government-issued money through a system he created and called *bitcoin*. He has proven that a peer-to-peer decentralized value exchange can work and this newly-created network slowly started changing the world. However, it is not bitcoin *per se* that changed the world. Nakamoto has successfully intertwined four crucial technologies that made the creation of bitcoin and other cryptocurrencies possible. These are the bitcoin protocol, consensus rules, proof-of-work, and blockchain.

The bitcoin protocol enables computers to communicate with the bitcoin network. Consensus rules enable the growth of the bitcoin network without a central authority. Proof-of-work gives uncompromising security to the network. Moreover, the blockchain enables the transparency and immutability of transaction records. These technologies created a system that made the exchange of value between and among peers without trusting any centralized intermediary possible.

In this article, we will focus on the importance of blockchain and smart contracts in creating a world where transactions are entirely automated and trustless.

The Blockchain Ecosystem 101

The blockchain is a recording system, which combined with other novel technologies, created the fundamental technology behind bitcoin and other cryptocurrencies. This unique record-keeping model accumulates transactions per block, which are then cryptographically-linked creating a "chain of transaction blocks."

To simplify, let us assume you are one of the several thousand record-keepers (nodes) in a cryptocurrency network. As a record-keeper, you maintain a copy of the records (blockchain) that have been checked by verifiers (miners). The verifiers authenticate and accumulate pieces of papers containing various transactions from a pool of unconfirmed transactions. Subsequently, verified transactions are placed in a box (block). The verifiers then compete in a complex mathematical race staking their computing power to win the right to place their box into the blockchain (i.e., proof-of-work).

Once a verifier wins the race, the winner's box of transactions is officially entered in the blockchain and is rewarded with freshly generated currency (e.g., bitcoins). All record-keepers in the network, including you, then add the winning verifier's box of verified transactions to the blockchain. Thus, the blockchain is a collection of verified transactions.

As record-keepers, you need to ensure that the blocks are in order before adding it to your copy of the blockchain. It may seem a very tedious and time-consuming process, but all of these have been properly compiled in a rulebook called *consensus rules*, and implemented through a protocol that makes it easy for computers to interact with the network and do the verification activities efficiently.

Blockchain: trustless and immutable

As you may glean from above, the blockchain is a major component of a highly-secure and decentralized system. The system is highly-secure because transactions have to undergo several layers of verification by independent parties (miners and nodes) who contribute significant amounts of computing power and energy to verify and secure the network. It is also decentralized because there are potentially thousands of participants (peers) that make the system work without a single, central authority or organization that makes decisions for the entire ecosystem. This is the reason why implementations of public blockchains are often called *trustless* since you do not have to trust anybody; instead, you put your trust in the entire network.

The blockchain is also considered *immutable* – meaning it is permanent; it cannot be changed. It is not completely unchangeable, but it will require enormous amounts of computing power to be able to make changes in the blockchain. This is because each block is linked to a chain that contains accumulated proof-of-work. If you wish to change a transaction, say, made last week, you need to have more than half of the equivalent computing power spent by the miners previous week to have it changed. Currently, the computing power required to make this possible is around 20 million tera hashes per second (TH/s). This will require you to set up an entire warehouse of specialized mining equipment called *application specific integrated circuits* (ASIC) and spend millions of dollars' worth of electricity. Just imagine if you want to change a transaction that is more than one week old – the cost would be so staggering that it is better to leave it as it is. As more blocks are added on top of a block, the transactions in that block become difficult to modify. The bitcoin blockchain has been programmed to add a block every 10 minutes.

Blockchain is not Bitcoin

When people talk about bitcoin, they sometimes talk about the blockchain as its underlying technology. It is partly true because blockchain is one of the components of the core technology that makes bitcoin possible. This association usually leads people to conclude that blockchain can only be used to support bitcoin or other cryptocurrencies that are used as mediums of exchange.

The application of blockchain technology in the various digital currencies like bitcoin, litecoin, and monero is its first successful implementation. However, blockchain as a record-keeping mechanism is not limited to accounting for currency-related transactions. This was subsequently proven by a young Canadian programmer named Vitalik Buterin.

What is a smart contract?

In 2015, Buterin realized that the technology behind bitcoin has more potential. He then started building a new blockchain that can be used not only as a medium of exchange, but also as a platform for building applications. He envisioned a blockchain that can be used to share computing power – a decentralized application platform. At the core of this new blockchain, which is now known as Ethereum, is the concept of *smart contracts*.

Smart contract is not a new concept. Programmer and cryptographer Nick Szabo first introduced it in 1993. He described it as a *digital vending machine* where an input, any digital assets or representation of value, is placed in the machine. Once the machine verifies the input, it automatically drops something in exchange for the value placed. In this case, it may be a tangible or intangible good (e.g., a soda or subscription). In this illustration, the exchange of value is automatically done by the machine (smart contract) without human intervention.

A smart contract is similar to a signed contract wherein value is exchanged between parties but without the services of intermediaries, such as lawyers. It is then executed digitally by a computer program. Basically, smart contracts digitally facilitate, enforce, settle, and verify arrangements between parties exactly as programmed. This can significantly reduce the costs of creating, executing, and litigating contracts since you do not have to pay a lawyer to ensure that the other party will hold their end of the contract or blindly trust the other party to fulfill their obligation.

This is the beauty of smart contracts run on public blockchains: you do not need to trust the other party – you trust the entire network instead. If the other party fails to deliver, the smart contract automatically returns your payment, and possibly imposes a programmed punishment on the other party. Furthermore, smart contracts that run on public blockchain have no downtimes, cannot be censored, can easily be verified (trackable), and are essentially irreversible (immutable).

Smart contracts on Ethereum

The bitcoin blockchain made basic smart contracts possible. Although value can be exchanged between parties using consensus rules, time functions, multi-signatures, and hash functions, most of these contracts are limited to currency use cases.

In contrast, Buterin's creation, ethereum, was specifically designed to build decentralized applications using smart contracts. Ethereum's programming language called *solidity* opened up new opportunities for programmers to write their programs using the ethereum blockchain's computing power. These developers can pay for the use of ethereum's blockchain in *ether*, the ethereum's native currency.

One of the most common use cases of smart contracts on ethereum is *crowdfunding*. In an initial coin offering (ICO), the crypto-world's way of crowdfunding using cryptocurrencies, developers who want to pursue the development of their apps can easily raise funds using smart contracts. Investors in an ICO contribute cryptocurrencies, usually bitcoin and ether, in exchange for a project's *tokens*. These tokens are created using smart contracts. Often, the tokens will only be issued if certain project criteria are met, such as meeting a *soft cap* or the minimum investment raised, to proceed with the project. If the soft cap is not met, the smart contract automatically returns all bitcoin and ethers contributed by the investors. Else, the equivalent number of tokens will be released to the investors.

A new age of smart contracts

We are only beginning to see the possibilities of using smart contracts to solve existing real-world problems. The current database systems implemented by central authorities have had pervasive issues that smart contracts and blockchain can resolve.

Smart contracts on public blockchains have started disrupting the current financial ecosystem making banks less relevant to the use of smart contracts in escrow and settlement services. Medical records can be streamlined with healthcare service providers, insurance companies, and pharmacies, which will have relevant access to your records, without compromising your ability to maintain control over the management of these records. You can create a will using a smart contract, and the distribution of your assets will be automatically executed by your intentions only when your death is confirmed.

Land titles and gun records that are recorded on a public blockchain can easily be transferred between a buyer and seller using a smart contract, without spending much for the transfer. Governments or even smaller organizations can use smart contracts in voting systems to ensure accuracy and transparency that will preserve the integrity of the elections. CPU owners can earn extra cash by lending their idle computing power and storage to those who need it without going through a central electronic marketplace.

There are more applications of smart contracts on blockchains that are currently being tested, and it is certain that more will be discovered soon. We once again see a rush of interest (and funds) towards blockchain and smart contract projects similar to the time when internet usage started to grow in the 1990s. Just like the thousands of internet and mobile projects that have been presented to the public, many of these blockchain projects will also undoubtedly fail. Due to these failed projects, many famous people will brand blockchain as a "complete failure." Blockchains and smart contracts have many imperfections and disadvantages. However, just like the internet, which was once branded as a complete failure, developers will surely find ways to reduce these issues and make its application mainstream. Ultimately, smart contracts on blockchains will become disruptive drivers that will usher in a new age in our society.

So now, can you imagine a world where transactions are executed without trust?

Scam Checklist

Bitcoin and cryptocurrency are relatively new concepts. They are also quite tricky to grasp. Because of these reasons, 'cryptocurrency' is the latest scam idea for fraudsters, who use the public's lack of understanding, to defraud others.

Here is a quick checklist to help you identify an investment scam posing as a legitimate cryptocurrency project.

☐ The promise of high "guaranteed" returns
☐ Agents/representatives have difficulty in explaining how the cryptocurrency solves an existing problem
☐ Advertised as "risk-free"
☐ Sales agents have high commissions
☐ Bonus for 'inviting' new investors
☐ Has an existing scam warning
☐ No whitepaper
☐ Unknown founders or core development team
☐ No online platform or website
☐ No blockchain engineer or developer in the team
☐ Unclear token or coin economics (supply analysis)
☐ No token or coin wallet
☐ No active online community or forum on developer websites

If you have ticked one or two items above, you need to conduct a more in-depth study of the cryptocurrency project being offered to you. Remember that most cryptocurrency projects are decentralized, so there should be no sales agents or representatives soliciting investments from the public.

If you have ticked more than three items above, it is highly probable that you are dealing with an investment scam.

As long as you do not understand the model behind any cryptocurrency project, it is best to avoid investing in them.